2

THE
KING'S BOOK
of
NUMEROLOGY

Volume 10

HISTORIC ICONS

Part 1

RICHARD ANDREW KING

© by Richard Andrew King
Published by Richard King Publications
PO Box 3621
Laguna Hills, CA 92654

This King's Numerology[tm] system is neither intended to extol nor defame any featured individual, whether named or unnamed. Its purpose is to show the relationship between people's lives and their numbers in order to further the understanding of numerology as a science and the King's Numerology[tm] system in particular.

Library of Congress Cataloging-in-Publication Data
King, Richard Andrew
The King's Book of Numerology, Volume 10: Historic Icons – Part 1
ISBN: 978-0-931872-25-9 Pricing: 90000
Date of Publication: 26 October 2017

DEDICATION

Much love and gratitude to my daughters—Christa and Chandra,
for their undying assistance, love, devotion and support of my work.

ACKNOWLEDGMENTS

Many thanks to . . .

Adam "Frog" Mahan for his development of the book's cover

and

Lewis Hunter Stowers III for his artistic expertise

DISCLAIMER

This work is neither designed to extol nor defame any of the subjects featured. Its purpose is simply to compare, contrast and correlate the numbers of their birth dates and birth names with their destinies of fame and fortune in order to enlighten the public to the truth and reality of numerology as a science and art.

PHOTO ATTRIBUTION

All photos in this work are courtesy of Wikimedia Commons and Google images.

Richard Andrew King

RICHARD ANDREW KING – BOOKS

Available through RichardKing.net and major online retailers.

KBN Series:

1. *The King's Book of Numerology: Volume I – Foundations & Fundamentals*

2. *The King's Book of Numerology II: Forecasting – Part 1*

3. *The King's Book of Numerology 3: Master Numbers*

4. *The King's Book of Numerology 4: Intermediate Principles*

5. *The King's Book of Numerology 5: IR Sets – Level 1*

6. *The King's Book of Numerology 6: Love Relationships*

7. *The King's Book of Numerology 7: Parenting Wisdom – Numerology & Life Truths*

8. *The King's Book of Numerology 8: Forecasting – Part 2*

9. *The King's Book of Numerology 9: Numeric Biography, Princess Diana*

10. *The King's Book of Numerology 10: Historic Icons – Part 1*

Numerology books published separately . . .

The Age of the Female – A Thousand Years of Yin

Your Love Numbers – Discovering The Secrets of Your Life, Loves & Relationships (KBN6)

Destinies of the Rich & Famous – The Secret Numbers of Extraordinary Lives

Parenting Wisdom for the 21st Century – Raising Your Children By Their Numbers To Achieve Their Highest Potential (KBN7)

Blueprint of a Princess – Diana Frances Spencer, Queen of Hearts (KBN9)

Non-Numerology books . . .

Messages from the Masters – Timeless Truths for Spiritual Seekers

The Black Belt Book of Life – Secrets of a Martial Arts Master

The Karate Consciousness – From Worldly Warrior to Mystic Master

Parenting Wisdom – What to Teach the Children

The Age of the Female II – Heroines of the Shift

The Galactic Transcripts

99 Poems of the Spirit

THE KING'S BOOK OF NUMEROLOGY

Volume 10

HISTORIC ICONS – Part 1

TABLE OF CONTENTS

Richard Andrew King

NUMBER POWER

© Richard Andrew King

Numbers tell the time;
as well, they tell the tale;
numbers calculate the voyage
of life in its detail.

Numbers, just like coins,
incorporate two sides –
positive and negative,
as in the turn of tides.

Numbers are the codes of life;
they gauge, describe, define
the framework and the structure
of a life that is divine.

Numbers are life's basis
and, as cosmic law avers,
the blueprint of our destiny
has its design in numbers.

AUTHOR'S INTRODUCTION

This book has one purpose—to illustrate the veritable relationship between an individual's destiny and his or her numbers using The King's Numerology^{tm} system.

Each of us is born into this world with a blueprint of our life that is based solely on our full birth name and birth date. This may seem unbelievable, but it is true! This books reveals the secret association between life and numbers.

The individuals featured herein are famous and historic individuals. The reason for this is quite simple—the lives and histories of famous people are known and accessible. Therefore, it is easy to correlate their numbers with the circumstances, conditions, events, issues and challenges of their lives.

Each of the subjects will be treated in general terms, and although each featured individual's life is worthy of a full book, this work will highlight only those aspects of their destinies that are commonly known and of interest.

Because each of the subjects is unique, their charts will be different. However, when their numbers are presented and compared with their lives, the validity of the relationship between their numbers and their destinies will be indisputably apparent.

Once we see the relationship between the lives of these featured icons and their full names and birth dates, it will revolutionize our lives. How could it not? Life is not happenstance. There is a Power at work formulating our destinies that transcends human comprehension, a Power so vast and intelligent that we cannot but be humbled by its Reality.

Life is numbers. A simple scan of the Periodic Table of Elements reveals that every element is known by both a letter label and a number. Oxygen, for example, has a letter designation of "O" and a numerical equivalent of 8. When we breathe, we don't think we're inhaling Os and 8s but in one sense we are. So it is with our lives and destinies. They are also designated by letters and

Richard Andrew King

numbers. Letters form words, so words are important because they house energies, just like every element houses its own specific energy. In effect, words are more than units of language. They are energy indicators.

As we shall discuss, master numbers (multiple numbers of the same single number) are powerful, such as 11-555-8888. The most powerful binary number indicating universality and public exposure is the master number 99. While not all of our featured icons have the 99 in their charts, many do.

Because this work features celebrities, it is an interesting side note that the specific numerological value of the word "Celebrity" is a 99 – the master number of great public exposure, universality and being known to the masses!

This is a "stand alone" book. It is not necessary to have read or studied other King's Numerology[tm] works to enjoy this work. Still, beginning, intermediate and advanced numerology students will garner much knowledge from the case studies of the famous individuals featured here in KBN10.

I hope you will find this journey into the lives of these historic iconic individuals educational, enlightening and edifying. It is a marvelous journey of mystery and unprecedented discovery. As the charts of our featured icons reveal, not only is life destined but so are fame and fortune!

To the Inner Secrets of Life and Destiny,

Richard Andrew King

PREFACE A

FOUNDATIONS OF FAME

Have you ever wondered why rich and famous people are rich and famous? This book is going to reveal the secret truth behind the remarkable destinies of twelve of the most recognizable and famous people known to the modern world —

- Dr. Albert Einstein
- Amelia Earhart
- Elvis Presley
- General George Patton
- Howard Hughes
- John F. Kennedy
- Marilyn Monroe
- Michael Jackson
- Muhammad Ali
- Oprah Winfrey
- Princess Diana
- Sarah Palin

This journey into the lives of these global icons is going to be fun, exciting, informative, educational and eye-opening. Not only will it reveal the secrets of their destinies, it will also give insight into what makes them tick or what made them tick, why they're special, each in their own way, and why they do the things they do or did do. It will also answer such questions as . . .

Richard Andrew King

- What made Dr. Albert Einstein a great scientist?

- What drove Oprah Winfrey to be a media queen?

- Why was Princess Diana so loved, yet so hounded by the press?

- Why was Marilyn Monroe such a gifted but troubled actress?

- What connects Princess Diana to Marilyn Monroe?

- Why was Howard Hughes such an eccentric rich recluse?

- What drove Amelia Earhart to explore and fly the world?

- What was the cause of Michael Jackson's rise and fall?

- Why did George Patton become a uniquely powerful general?

- Why was Elvis Presley such a dominate and dynamic star?

- What connects John F. Kennedy's life to his assassination?

- What drove Muhammad Ali to be a loquacious boxing legend?

- What is the primary reason for Sarah Palin's popularity?

This is just a sampling of the questions this book will answer in ways never before known or considered. Using a very simple process, the enormous success and fame of these iconic individuals will be revealed through the King's Numerology^{tm}, the divine science of numbers and their relationship to life and destiny.

The naked truth this book is going to share with you may seem unbelievable, incomprehensible, unacceptable, perhaps even ridiculous. Yet, the reality is, unequivocally, that success, wealth, fame and fortune are based in one thing and one thing only . . . destiny. Any individuals who are rich and famous, whether in this age or any age, were destined to be so from the very beginning of their lives. In fact, the blueprint of their destinies was created before they ever exited their mother's womb! This truth is clearly visible in the numerology charts of those individuals featured here. As you will soon come to understand, fact is stranger than fiction, and the fact of life is that success, wealth, fame and fortune are neither happenstance nor a matter of luck. They are all predetermined. People are born into fame and fortune.

Following is a brief list of powerful and impressive quotations from esteemed individuals, sacred texts, mystics and saints endorsing the principle of a predetermined existence. Although the concept of a destined or fated life may seem questionable to mankind as a whole, it certainly is not questionable to those possessing higher knowledge of the spiritual cosmos.

DESTINY – QUOTES

Everything is determined, the beginning as well as the end, by forces over which we have no control. It is determined for the insect, as well as for the star. Human beings, vegetables or cosmic dust - we all dance to a mysterious tune, intoned in the distance by an invisible piper.
~ Dr. Albert Einstein

Fame comes only when deserved, and then is as inevitable as destiny, for it is destiny.

~ Henry Wadsworth Longfellow

There is no such thing as chance, and what seems to us merest accident springs from the deepest source of destiny. ~ Johann Friedrich Von Schiller

To every thing there is a season, and a time to every purpose under the heaven.

~ The Bible: Ecclesiastes 3:1-8

The very hairs of your head are all numbered.

~ The Bible: St. Matthew 10:30

All men come into this world with a destiny of their own which goes on pushing them relentlessly on the course already marked out for them.

~ Saint Charan Singh, 20th Century

Richard Andrew King

God himself forces his creatures into destined paths of karmas (fruits of previous actions) over which they have no control and which cannot be effaced. Whatever is destined to take place must take place. ~ Guru Amardas-15th/16th Centuries

No living man can send me to the shades before my time; no man of woman born, coward or brave, can shun his destiny. ~ Homer - *The Iliad*

If a man is destined to drown, he will drown even in a spoonful of water.

~ Yiddish Proverb

A consistent soul believes in destiny, a capricious one in chance.

~ Benjamin Disraeli

The Unknowable Lord's pen inscribes the destinies of all beings on their foreheads.
~ Granth Sahib - Sikhism

He that is born to be hanged shall never be drowned. ~ French Proverb

What God writes on your forehead you will become. ~ The Koran

The real test of a man is not how well he plays the role he has invented for himself, but how well he plays the role that destiny assigned to him.

~ Jan Patočka - Czech Philosopher

Destiny Commands --- We Must Obey!   ~ Sir Winston Churchill

The total number of breaths which one is to take till death, the morsels which one is to eat and the steps which one is to walk are all preordained at birth and no one can alter, decrease or increase them.   ~ Saint Sawan Singh, 20th Century

Destiny is an absolutely definite and inexorable ruler.   ~ Aleister Crowley

Nothing can happen which is not in your destiny. ~ Saint Charan Singh, 20th Century

Our present life is already determined before we are born. What destiny has planned for you will come to pass without any planning on your part. Your destiny will cause you to act and make effort according to its plan. Old age, health, poverty, richness, sickness, disease, wealth, learning, honor, dishonor and time of death are all pre-ordained while a man is in the womb of his mother, so a wise man never worries or frets or regrets anything.   ~ Saint Jagat Singh, 20th Century

Nothing in nature is by chance. Something appears to be chance only because of our lack of knowledge.   ~ Baruch de Spinoza - Dutch Philosopher

Richard Andrew King

THE TWO FACTORS OF DESINTY

As human beings, our destinies are revealed by two factors:

1. Our date of birth

2. Our full name at birth

Incredible, isn't it, that our entire destinies are contained within our birth name and birth date? While this may seem inconceivable, let's recall the words of the man who is considered by many authorities to be the greatest scientific genius of all time, Sir Isaac Newton:

> *God created everything by number, weight and measure. It is the perfection of God's works that they are all done with the greatest simplicity. He is the God of order and not of confusion.*

Also to be equally considered are the words of the first pure mathematician, the famed Pythagoras:

> *Numbers rule the universe. Everything is arranged according to number and mathematical shape.*

These profound statements cannot be taken lightly. In fact, how much of our science today is directly related to their remarkable observations? Can we overlook Einstein's quote, *Everything is determined*? Can we dismiss Newton's observations that 1. *God created everything by number, weight and measure;* that His works are 2. *All done with the greatest simplicity* and 3. that *He is the God of order and not of confusion*? Can we deny the clear logic of Pythagoras when he noted, *Numbers rule the universe*? Given these profound statements by three of the most heralded scientists in history, would it be wise to reject the premise that each of our lives has a destiny and that the blueprint of that destiny is stated in the simple and ordered framework of the numbers associated with our full birth name and birth date? You be the judge as we take a journey into the lives and destinies of our twelve historic icons.

PREFACE B

THE KEYS OF FAME

Human beings are like snowflakes—they're generally the same but specifically different. The same is true for people who are rich and famous. Their lives are generally the same but specifically different. Therefore, in discussing each of our historic icons, we'll highlight those items in their King's Numerology™ charts which make them special using the following *Keys of Fame*.

- Single Numbers and Keywords

- Master Numbers

- Stacking

- Linkage

- Name Timeline

- Letter Timeline

- Basic Matrix

- Numeric Houses

- IR Sets

- Life Matrix

Richard Andrew King

SIMPLE LETTER VALUE CHART

Before we discuss the *Keys of Fame*, here is a quick note about the process of numerology. Numbers are the most universal communication system. Our destinies are comprised of both our birth date and birth name, so how are our names converted to numbers? Answer: by using the simple letter value chart below in which each group of letters (called genera) has a numerical value. To determine the numerical value of any name, we simply associate each letter of the name with its number, add them up and reduce to a single digit.

Simple Letter Value Chart									
[Each single number grouping is called a Genera]									
Letters	A	B	C	D	E	F	G	H	I
	J	K	L	M	N	O	P	Q	R
	S	T	U	V	W	X	Y	Z	&
Value	1	2	3	4	5	6	7	8	9

For example, the name "Kim" has a simple name value of 6.

K		I		M			
2	+	9	+	4	=	15	1 + 5 = **6**

The name "David" has a simple value of 4.

D		A		V		I		D			
4	+	1	+	4	+	9	+	4	=	22	2 + 2 = **4**

The name "Marie" has a simple value of 1.

M		A		R		I		E			
4	+	1	+	9	+	9	+	5	=	28	2 + 8 = 10 = **1**

Now, on to the *Keys of Fame*.

THE KEYS OF FAME

Following are the most dominant keys to assessing fame and fortune in a King's Numerology^{tm} chart. Each person's destiny is different from another. Therefore, as we discuss each person we'll highlight the specific keys which make his or her life stand out.

SINGLE NUMBERS AND KEYWORDS

Numbers are not simply arithmetic symbols. They are also labels for certain attributes, characteristics and energy fields. A very brief list of *keywords* for each single number is described in the following chart to give you an idea of what each number represents. For a more expansive list of keywords and phrases, see Appendix 1 at the back of the book (page 231).

Single Numbers and a Sampling of Their Keywords

1   self, ego, masculine, identity, independence, action, authority, solo, logical

2   others, feminine, relationship, support, dependence, reaction, emotion, illogical

3   self-expression, image(s), well-being, art, pleasure, words, children, fulfillment, joy

4   order, organization, work, service, security, stability, routine, convention, roots

5   freedom/slavery, detachment, movement, motion, the senses, non-convention, variety

6   personal love, family, domicile, community, devotion, duty, nurturing, support

7   thought, thinker, study, reclusion, introspection, analysis, wisdom, internalization

8   connection, interaction, management, engagement, orchestration, externalization

9   power, universality, public stage, philanthropy, education, broadcasting, mankind

Richard Andrew King

MASTER NUMBERS

Master numbers are multiple digit numbers of the same single cipher such as 11, 333, or 7777. Like nuclear energy, they are extremely powerful in both their positive and negative aspects. The more master numbers present in a chart, the more power a person's life exhibits—constructively or destructively. Most of the master numbers we'll be discussing will be the two digit variety. Following is a brief list of each master number and a few of its keywords.

11 *Master Aspirant/Achiever*—inspirational, intense, others-oriented

22 *Master Builder*—loves to construct, organize, develop, build

33 *Master Imaginator/Communicator*—artistic, creative, words, sex

44 *Master Worker/Leader*—generals, executives, managers, leaders

55 *Master Explorer/Creator*—extremely original, unique, rebel

66 *Master Lover/Artisan*—loving expression, communication, words

77 *Master Thinker/Revolutionary*—freedom oriented, stands alone

88 *Master Interactor/Spiritual Master*—connective, deep, substantive

99 *Master Performer/Master's Master*—universal, dominant, known

STACKING

Stacking is the simultaneous occurrence of the same number, numbers, or number patterns in a chart. Stacking creates intensity, just as multiple heaters create more heat than one heater. For example, a person may have the master number 33 appear simultaneously in three different places in a chart or they may have a number pattern such as an 11-2 appear simultaneously in multiple places. Both are examples of stacking.

LINKAGE

Linkage (or *Linking*) is the continual or repetitive occurrence of the same number or number patterns within a chart. Linking creates continuity. *Life linkage* is when the same numbers or patterns occur in a chart from birth to death.

For example, the day, month and year of a person's birth are called *Epochs*. They each denote lengths of time, i.e., *timelines*. If a person were born on the 3rd of March, there would be linkage because the day, the 3rd (and its timeline), would continue through the month of March, the third month (and its timeline). In contrast, were a person born on the third of February, there would be no linkage because the same number does not continuously occur; the day, a 3, is followed by the month of February, a 2. To further our example, if a person were born on the 3rd of March in the year 2001 (a 3 in reduction), there would be *life linkage* throughout the entire life from birth to death because the simple format would be 3-3-3 (day-3; month-3; year-3).

As we will see in our famous individuals, many of them have *stacking*, *linking* or both in their charts, thus creating the intensity and continuity needed to generate great fame and fortune. In review, *stacking* creates intensity and *linking* creates continuity. Together, they help generate long term power, resulting in powerful lives and destinies.

NAME TIMELINE

A person's full name creates his *Name Timeline*. The full name is further subdivided into timelines of each of the names comprising the full name. Each name, whether the full name or the individual names of the full name, represents characteristics as well as periods of time. For example, if a person's birth name were "John Doe," it would have its own timeline and then each of the separate names "John" and "Doe" would also have their own timelines describing specific time periods in the life of John.

As a note, our birth names are neither random nor accidental. Created by higher powers, they are part of the divine plan given to each of us through our parents to fulfill our destiny.

Richard Andrew King

LETTER TIMELINE

The *Letter Timeline* reflects the importance of each letter of the full name and each of its separate names. Letters, like names, represent a specific period of time (timeline) as well as specific attributes.

For example, in the name "John Doe," each of the letters has a time period and value corresponding to its number in the Simple Letter Value Chart. In this case, "J" (the 10th letter of the alphabet becoming a 1 in reduction: $1 + 0 = 1$) lasts for a period of one year and represents the characteristics of the 1: self, ego, independence, identity, action, will power, male energy and new beginnings. The "O" (the 15th letter of the alphabet) will last for six years ($1 + 5 = 6$) because that is its simple value. It will address issues of the 6: love, home, romance, community, beauty, nurturing and harmony in its positive aspect, or it will, perhaps, reflect the negative side of its coin: hate, jealously, envy, bitterness, anger. The "H" will last for eight years and will manifest energies of the 8: connection, interaction, orchestration, management and social power. The "N" (the 14th letter of the alphabet – a 5 in reduction) of "John" will last for five years indicating attributes of the number 5: change, movement, motion, loss, detachment, freedom, uncertainty. When the numbers comprising the spelling of the word "John," which are 1-6-8-5, are added together, the result is 20. Therefore, the name "John" has a twenty year timeline, beginning at birth and continuing through the twentieth year.

The *Name Timeline* (NTL) and *Letter Timeline* (LTL) are dramatic aspects in a numerology chart because they reflect the most direct energy of an individual. Oftentimes, a person's fortunes and misfortunes are more clearly depicted in the NTL and LTL than anywhere else in a chart.

BASIC MATRIX

The *Basic Matrix* is a general numeric profile of a person and his destiny. It is comprised of eight components, each component identified by a number as seen in the *Simple Basic Matrix Grid* below. Lifepath (LP), Expression (Exp), Performance/Experience (PE), Soul (S), Material Soul (MS), Nature (N), Material Nature (MN) and Voids (V).

Simple Basic Matrix Grid

Lifepath	Expression	PE	Soul	M/S	Nature	M/N	Voids
#	#	#	#	#	#	#	#

Sample of a Simple Basic Matrix Grid with Numbers

Lifepath	Expression	PE	Soul	M/S	Nature	M/N	Voids
5	3	8	9	5	3	8	7 & 8

A brief description of each Basic Matrix component follows.

BASIC MATRIX COMPONENTS AND DESCRIPTIONS

Basic Matrix Component	Brief Description
Expression — Exp. (full birth name)	The person as actor or actress, full potentials, assets and liabilities
Lifepath — LP (birth date)	The life script, path in life, lessons to learn (positive/negative), energy world
Performance/Experience — PE (Expression plus Lifepath)	The role the person will play on life's stage; the performance given
Soul (derived from the Expression vowels: A-E-I-O-U-Y)	Primary desires, needs, wants, motivations
Material Soul – MS (Soul plus Lifepath)	Secondary desires, needs, wants, motivations
Nature (derived from the Expression consonants)	Primary personality and manner of doing things
Material Nature – MN (Nature plus Lifepath)	Worldly personality and manner of doing things
Voids	Missing numbers in the birth name

Richard Andrew King

NUMERIC HOUSES

Numeric Houses represent the numbers 1 through 9 associated with the letters in the full birth name. The value of each number can play a significant role in the destiny. Houses correspond to genera (letter groupings). Therefore, the 1st House represents the number 1 and its attributes of independence, identity, self, ego, action, logic and male energy. It is comprised of the letters A-J-S. The 2nd House represents the number 2 and its attributes of relationship, others, teamwork, dependence, emotion and female energy. This can be depicted in the following chart.

House	Letters	Attributes
1st	A-J-S	Self, ego, independence, identity, action, males, reason (fire sign)
2nd	B-K-T	Others, dependence, relationship, females, emotion (water sign)
3rd	C-L-U	Children, health, well-being, image, words, expression (air sign)
4th	D-M-V	Work, service, security, stability, convention, roots (earth sign)
5th	E-N-W	Freedom, diversity, motion, non-convention, wings (fire sign)
6th	F-O-X	Family, love, romance, domesticity, nurturing, heart (water sign)
7th	G-P-Y	Internalization, analysis, examination, solitude, thought (air sign)
8th	H-Q-Z	Externalization, commerce, status, interaction, flow (earth sign)
9th	I-R	Universality, public arena, expansion, endings (all elements)

INFLUENCE/REALITY SETS (IR SETS)

The Influence/Reality Set (IR Set for short) is a numeric structure illustrating the Influence ("I") and Reality ("R") of specific energies in a chart. The *Influence* can be considered the *cause* and the *Reality* the *effect* or *outcome* of a condition, event, or circumstance. Basically, the IR set gives general ideas as to how a person will react to certain stimuli or events in his or her life. IR sets are major players in understanding destiny. The simple format of the IR Set represents two numbers – the Influencing number/energy and the Reality number/energy. For a thorough study of IR Sets, study *The King's Book of Numerology II – Forecasting, Part 1* (aka, KBN2).

VOIDS

Voids are missing numbers in the full birth name of the individual. If a person's name has no As, Js, or Ss, he has a 1 void. If his name has no Bs, Ks, or Ts, he has a 2 void and so forth. Voids represent areas of focused effort, attention and concern related to their numbers. They can be problematic, potentially creating havoc in a person's life, especially if located in a Challenge position. Sometimes, however, voids force a person to concentrate on the areas of their attributes, thus filling up the hole they represent and giving meaning and purpose to a person's life.

LIFE MATRIX

The *Life Matrix* is the numeric grid illustrating timelines, general influences and outcomes of a person's life from birth to death based on the birth date of the individual. In essence, the Life Matrix is the internal framework of the Lifepath. If the Lifepath were likened to a train ride across the United States, for example, the Life Matrix components would be the different states, climates and geographical areas the train would pass through in its journey from start to finish. The *Life Matrix* is comprised of three ingredients: Epochs, Pinnacles, Challenges.

1. *Epochs* are components of the birth date: *day*, *month*, *year*. We can think of Epochs as continual energy fields within the Lifepath itself. Their timelines are generally longer than Pinnacles and Challenges. If a person were born on 8 July 2000, the first Epoch would be an 8, the second Epoch would be a 7 (July is the 7th calendar month) and the third Epoch would be a 2. The first two Epochs are 27 years in length; the third Epoch begins at age 55 and terminates at death.

2. *Pinnacles* are derived from *addition* of the Epochs. They are activities which are generally known or viewable to the outside world and which pull us forward.

First Pinnacle: add day and month

Ex: 8 July creates a 6 Pinnacle (8 + 7 = 15: 1 + 5 = 6)

Second Pinnacle: add month and year of birth

Ex. July 2000 creates a 9 Pinnacle (7 + 2 = 9)

Richard Andrew King

Third Pinnacle: add the first and second Pinnacles together

Ex. $6 + 9 = 15$: $1 + 5 = 6$

Fourth Pinnacle: add the day of birth to the year of birth

Ex. $8 + 2 = 10$: $1 + 0 = 1$

3. *Challenges* are derived from *subtraction* of the Epochs. They reveal personal areas of focus, friction and toil which are not generally known to the outside world.

First Challenge: subtract day and month from each other

Ex: $8 - 7 = 1$

Second Challenge: subtract month and year

Ex: $7 - 2 = 5$ (2000 reduced to a single digit)

Third Challenge: subtract 1st and 2nd Challenges

Ex: $5 - 1 = 4$

Four Challenge: subtract the day of birth from the year

Ex: $8 - 2 = 6$

Note: This is a simple explanation of the Challenge process, which has greater complexity than explained here. For more information read: *The King's Book of Numerology II: Forecasting – Part I.*

Following is the Life Matrix grid we'll be using for illustration during the purposes of revealing the destinies of our featured individuals. It is a major piece of the destiny puzzle. We will adjust it for each of our subjects, highlighting certain features and making a few notes about their destinies.

LIFE MATRIX

		4th/Crown Pinnacle	
* Pinnacles: derived by addition		3rd/Grand Pinnacle	
	1st Pinnacle		2nd Pinnacle

1st Epoch (Day)	2nd Epoch (Month)	3rd Epoch (Year)

	1st Challenge		2nd Challenge
* Challenges: derived by subtraction		3rd/Grand Challenge	
		4th/Crown Challenge	

Now that we've explained the *Keys of Fame*, let's begin our journey into the destinies of these historic individuals and see how their remarkable lives are a reflection of their numbers. Our first featured person has, perhaps, the most unique numerology chart of the subjects in this book. He is none other than the most famous scientist of the Twentieth Century, Dr. Albert Einstein.

Richard Andrew King

HISTORIC ICON #1

ALBERT EINSTEIN

Born: Albert Einstein – 14 March 1879

Died – 18 April 1955, age 76

----

* *Time* Person of the Twentieth Century

* Regarded as the Father of Modern Physics

* Nobel Laureate, Physics - 1921

For his services to theoretical physics, and especially

for his discovery of the law of the photoelectric effect

[Nobelprize.org]

(Photo courtesy of Wikimedia Commons)

Richard Andrew King

It is appropriate that this work begins with Dr. Albert Einstein because it was he who powerfully proclaimed . . .

> *Everything is determined, the beginning as well as the end, by forces over which we have no control. It is determined for the insect, as well as for the star. Human beings, vegetables or cosmic dust – we all dance to a mysterious tune, intoned in the distance by an invisible piper.*

Everything is determined, says the greatest scientist of the Twentieth Century . . . and everything includes fame as well as fortune. This is the crux of the matter. Fame and fortune <u>are</u> <u>not</u> accidental. People are born into them. Fame and fortune may be in their stars but as we shall see, fame and fortune are most definitely in their numbers!

MASTER NUMBERS IN EINSTEIN'S CHART

Einstein was an amazing individual. Of this there is no doubt, but what made him amazing? The answer is, in part, that not only does his King's Numerology[tm] chart contain every master number (11 to 99), Einstein's Life Matrix of Epochs, Pinnacles and Challenges contains at least one master number in every component!

Additionally, the only master number missing in Einstein's Life Matrix is the number 33 but his Lifepath itself is a 33 and since the Life Matrix is the framework (the inner structure) of the Lifepath, it can be said that Einstein's entire Lifepath, as determined by his date of birth, contains every master number: 11-22-33-44-55-66-77-88-99. Einstein's chart is, without question, a most incredible and powerful numerology chart. It is anything but usual and, in fact, is highly unusual.

Master Numbers in Albert Einstein's Chart	
11	Nature
	Name Timeline (NTL) PE of "Einstein"
	1st Challenge
	1st Challenge PE
	3rd Challenge (Grand/Core)
	3rd Challenge PE
	4th Challenge (Crown)
	4th Challenge PE
22	Expression of "Albert"
	Material Soul
	2nd Challenge
	2nd Challenge PE
33	Lifepath
44	Material Nature
	1st Pinnacle PE
55	Name Timeline (NTL) PE of "Albert"
	2nd Pinnacle PE
66	4th Pinnacle PE (Crown)
	2nd Epoch PE
77	1st Epoch PE
88	3rd Epoch PE
99	3rd Pinnacle PE (Grand/Core)

Richard Andrew King

LIFE MATRIX
Voids: 4-6-7-8
ALBERT EINSTEIN
14 MARCH 1879

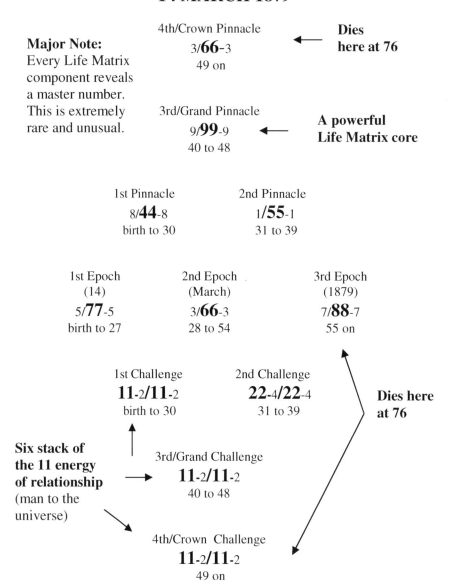

4th/Crown Pinnacle
3/**66**-3
49 on

← **Dies here at 76**

Major Note:
Every Life Matrix component reveals a master number. This is extremely rare and unusual.

3rd/Grand Pinnacle
9/**99**-9
40 to 48

← **A powerful Life Matrix core**

1st Pinnacle
8/**44**-8
birth to 30

2nd Pinnacle
1/**55**-1
31 to 39

1st Epoch
(14)
5/**77**-5
birth to 27

2nd Epoch
(March)
3/**66**-3
28 to 54

3rd Epoch
(1879)
7/**88**-7
55 on

1st Challenge
11-2/**11**-2
birth to 30

2nd Challenge
22-4/**22**-4
31 to 39

Dies here at 76

Six stack of the 11 energy of relationship (man to the universe)

3rd/Grand Challenge
11-2/**11**-2
40 to 48

4th/Crown Challenge
11-2/**11**-2
49 on

ALBERT EINSTEIN: BASIC MATRIX GRID

Basic Matrix: Albert Einstein

LP	Exp.	PE	Soul	MS	Nature	MN	Voids
33-6	9	6	7	22-4	11-2	44-8	4-6-7-8

Einstein's Basic Matrix shows his 33-6 Lifepath. The 6 is a result of simply adding the two 3s of the 33. This 33 in his Lifepath is the only master number not showing in his Life Matrix but the Life Matrix is contained within the 33-6 Lifepath itself, reflecting life lessons of love and hate, family, home, community, nation, self-expression, words and communication.

Einstein's 33-6 Lifepath is expressed in a multiplicity of ways, as witnessed in his marriages and family life, Jewish community ties, citizenships of different countries (Germany, Switzerland, Austria and the United States), the publication of hundreds of books and articles, as well as his speaking tours and events throughout his life. This 33 master energy of communication is strongly reinforced by his 3rd/Grand Pinnacle of 9 with its 99 master number PE which powerfully placed him and his life's work in the global arena and on the public stage of mankind.

Also corroborating Einstein's 33-6 Lifepath within his Life Matrix is the *stacking* of his 3/66-3 4th Crown Pinnacle IR set and 3/66-3 2nd Epoch IR set. The numbers 3-6-9 comprise the *Artistic Triad*. One of the reasons Einstein's chart is so powerful is that his chart reveals a *Master Artistic Triad* of 33-66-99 with the 66 being *stacked*.

Adding to the power of this Artistic Triad are his 9 Expression (giving him a global and charismatic persona) and his 6 PE. All this 3-6-9 energy creates an extremely powerful life of self-expression and communication.

Einstein's Soul is a 7. This gives him an intense desire to ask questions, have an enquiring mind and spirit, analyze, investigate, research, study, teach, inform, reflect, introspect and seek knowledge. A perfect pictorial and sculptural example of the 7 Soul energy is Rodin's universally famous marble and bronze statue, *The Thinker*. It typifies what the 7 Soul does—ask questions, analyze, examine, reflect, think and ponder deeply.

Einstein's 22-4 Material Soul (MS) illustrates that the depth of his thinking plays itself out in the area of order, design, structure, function, form, building, models and mechanics. This is strengthened in his 22/22 2nd Challenge. Additionally, Einstein's 44-8 Material Nature integrates the 22-4's structural energy into operating systems, functional mechanics and understanding the interconnection and flow between ideas and their manifestation and completion. This 44-8 master energy occupies Einstein's 1st Pinnacle PE.

What is also interesting regarding Einstein's Basic Matrix is that his four voids (4-6-7-8) are all contained within the Basic Matrix itself. The 4 void is contained within his 4 Material Soul; the 6 void occupies his Lifepath; the 7 void rules his Soul and the 8 void is centered in his 8 Material Nature. When a void is located in the Basic Matrix itself it can lessen any negative effects the voided number may have if it were to appear elsewhere in a chart. Therefore, it is a good thing that Einstein's voids are contained within his Basic Matrix.

NAME TIMELINE

The First name, "Albert"

As if there weren't enough master number energy in Einstein's Basic Matrix and Life Matrix, his Name Timeline also reveals the powerful energy of the 55-1 Master Explorer/Revolutionary number. The name "Albert" is a 22-4 Master Builder energy. We already know this 22-4 exists in his Material Soul and also as a double master dyad of 22-4/22-4 in the second Challenge of his Life Matrix, thus creating a quadstack (four stack) of 22-4 energy. When this 22 of "Albert" is added to his 33 Lifepath, the result is the 55-1 master number in the outcome part of the IR (Influence/Reality) set. This combination could be written as 22-4/55-1 which filters through the 33 Lifepath, so it could be written as 22-4/(33-6)/55-1. The 22-4/55-1 combination signifies massive unique and pioneering developments (55-1) in the realm of design, order, form, work, mechanics, structure and service (22-4). Additionally, the 55-1 energy also occupies Einstein's second Pinnacle from age 31 to 39, which brings us to an important note regarding Einstein's general theory of relativity. Note the 22-4/(33-6)/55-1 master triad of his *Albert* Name Timeline.

Name Timeline (NTL): Albert Einstein			
	First	Last	
	Albert	Einstein	
Names	Albert	Einstein	
Timeline	birth to 22	23 to 63	names recycle at age 64 beginning with Albert
General	22	41	
NTL	22-4/(33-6)/55-1	5	
IR Set		11-2	
Master #s	22-4 (Albert)/(33-6 LP)/55-1	11	

General Theory of Relativity

Nothing happens arbitrarily in the universe. As we've read, Einstein himself stated, *Everything is determined*. Well, as it just so happens, it was during Einstein's 2nd Pinnacle/Challenge period from ages 31 to 39 in the years 1910 to 1918 that he completed his work on the General Theory of Relativity, obviously a powerful concept.

As numbers reveal the destiny of one's life, the amalgam of master numbers of Einstein's life at that time support not only his work but his destiny. It was during this time that the master number of form and design—the 22-4, appeared as a quadstack (amalgam of four) in his chart accompanied by a double stack of 55-1 energy! It is predominately this combination of master energy, assisted by Einstein's other master numbers, that brought into reality his General Theory of Relativity.

This is not coincidence, and this is the purpose of this work—to reveal the connection between people's numbers and their destinies. When we see how all this fits together, it is impossible to deny the reality that life is destined—your life, my life, the lives of the rich and famous, the lives of the infamous and everyone who ever took a breath of life. When this reality is understood, it will revolutionize the way human beings live—if not collectively, then individually. In fact, perhaps this concept of our personal numbers reflecting our destiny can be labeled the *General Theory of Destiny* in keeping with the Einsteinian theme of the General Theory of Relativity.

Richard Andrew King

<u>The Second name, "Einstein"</u>

The name "Einstein" is a 5 in simple numbers. When this 5 is added to the 4 simple number of "Albert," the result is a 9, the number of universality and the public stage—the full Expression of "Albert Einstein."

When the 5 is added to his 6 Lifepath, the outcome is an 11, yet another master number. Therefore, the Name Timeline of "Einstein" would be written as 5/11-2; more fully as 5/(33-6)/11-2. When this 11 is combined with Einstein's 11 Nature in his Basic Matrix and each of the 11s in the three double-dyad Challenge components of his Life Matrix, Einstein has a whopping octostack (8 stack) of 11 energy designating inspiration and accomplishment in the realm of relationship. Relationship of space and time is the foundational theme of Einstein's work on general relativity.

EINSTEIN'S NOBEL PRIZE - 1921

Einstein won the Nobel Prize for physics in 1921 at age 42. The award was given for his discovery of the law of the photoelectric effect. There are three important connections with the Nobel Prize and his numbers.

First, when Einstein received his Prize at age 42 he was in his 3rd Pinnacle position between the ages of 40 and 48. The 3rd Pinnacle is also called the Grand Pinnacle or the Core Pinnacle. The IR set of Einstein's Grand Pinnacle is a 9/99-9; more fully as 9/(9)/99-9. This illustrates powerful recognition on the public stage. No number is more publically powerful than the 9 with a 9 Filter (his 9 Expression) and the resulting 99-9 outcome (9 + 9 =18 = 9). The results could not be more powerful. In very simple terms Einstein's Grand Pinnacle – the core of his 33-6 LP – is 9/(9)/9.

Second, Einstein's 3rd Challenge (also called the Grand or Core Challenge), which runs concurrently with his 3rd Pinnacle, is an 11-2/11-2 (more fully as 11-2/(9)/11-2, the energy of relationship in both Influence and Outcome positions. A person could have this numerical Challenge combination in their chart but not have the recognition that Einstein received because they might not have the 9/(9)/99-9 3rd Pinnacle IR set to accommodate the 11-2/(9)/11-2 energy in the Challenge.

Third, in the year of Einstein's Nobel Prize for Physics he was 42 years old. His life was transiting the "S" of "Ein<u>s</u>tein" in his Letter Timeline. The numerical pattern during this auspicious year was a 1/7 year, an IR set revealing actions (1) of the mind and its abilities (7) or the self (1) in isolation (7). This is the only 1/7 Letter Timeline period of Einstein's life except when he was one year of age. With the 33-6 LP Filter added, the broader IR Set would be 1/(33-6)/7.

This 1/7 Letter Timeline IR set is not that unusual. Any individual with a 6 Lifepath and an A, J or S in their name will experience this at some time in their life. However, combined with Einstein's Pinnacle/Challenge or PC Couplet of 9/99-9 (Pinnacle) and his 11-2/11-2 (Challenge), it is of note, adding to the numerical warp and woof, the fabric of Einstein's storied life.

SUMMARY

This brief numerical treatise regarding Albert Einstein's life is precisely that, brief. An entire book, even a volume of books, could easily be written on the numerological aspects of Einstein's life. However, the purpose of this book, as stated earlier, is not to completely detail the entire lives of its featured personalities but rather to simply highlight some of the main numerical correspondences between their destinies and their numbers solely based on their birth date and full name at birth to substantiate the truth of numbers and their relationship to life and destiny. Some of the amazing features of Albert Einstein's life are . . .

- The vast depth and breadth of *master numbers* in his King's Numerology[tm] chart, a chart not only containing every binary master number but revealing a Life Matrix that possesses every master number except the 33 which, although it did not appear in his Life Matrix, was in his Lifepath.
- The presence of a master number in every cell of his Life Matrix.
- The tristack of 11-2/11-2 IR set in his Challenge positions.
- His Core Pinnacle 9/99-9 IR set.
- The Master Artistic Triad (33-66-99): 33-6 Lifepath, 66-3 Crown Pinnacle PE and 2nd Epoch PE; 99-9 Grand Pinnacle PE.

Richard Andrew King

It is the conclusion of this brief treatise that the extreme amalgam of master numbers in his chart was, arguably, the main contributor in making Albert Einstein one of the most famous figures in history, as well as creating one of the most fascinating numerology charts of the destinies of the historic icons featured here in KBN10.

ALBERT EINSTEIN – QUOTES

Everything is determined, the beginning as well as the end, by forces over which we have no control. It is determined for the insect, as well as for the star. Human beings, vegetables or cosmic dust - we all dance to a mysterious tune, intoned in the distance by an invisible piper.

The goal is to raise the spiritual values of society.

A person starts to live when he can live outside himself.

Science without religion is lame, religion without science is blind.

The highest destiny of the individual is to serve rather than to rule.

Try not to become a man of success but rather to become a man of value.

Nothing will benefit human health and increase chances for survival of life on Earth as much as the evolution to a vegetarian diet.

The right to search for truth implies also a duty; one must not conceal any part of what one has recognized to be true.

The finest emotion of which we are capable is the mystic emotion.

Everyone who is seriously involved in the pursuit of science becomes convinced that a spirit is manifest in the laws of the Universe - a spirit vastly superior to that of man, and one in the face of which we, with our modest powers, must feel humble.

HISTORIC ICON #2

AMELIA EARHART

Born: Amelia Mary Earhart – 24 July 1897

Disappeared – 2 July 1937, age 39

(Declared legally dead in absentia, 5 January 1939, age 41)

----

* First woman to fly the Atlantic Ocean solo (1932, age 34)

* First woman to receive the U.S. Distinguished Flying Cross

~ United States Congress (1932)

* First person to fly the Pacific Ocean solo (1935, age 37)

* Disappeared mysteriously near Howland Island (1937, age 39)

(Photo courtesy of Wikimedia Commons)

Richard Andrew King

Amelia Mary Earhart was a woman of her time, before her time, in the time where women usually didn't do the daring deeds or have the 'daring do' of men. Earhart, a tomboy at heart, had courage and grit . . . and lots of it. She was a true pioneer and set many records in aviation. On 20 May 1932, on the 5th Anniversary of Charles Lindbergh's history-making flight, she became the first woman to fly solo across the Atlantic Ocean. For her heroics she was awarded the National Geographic Society's gold medal from President Herbert Hoover, and Congress awarded her the Distinguished Flying Cross—America's oldest military aviation award for gallantry. On 11 January 1935 she became the first person, not just a woman, to fly solo across the Pacific Ocean between Honolulu, Hawaii, and Oakland, California—an absolutely amazing feat for the time for anyone, man or woman. She was 37 (The Ninety-Nines, Inc.).

Distinguished Flying Cross—Congressional Citation

JOINT RESOLUTION: Authorizing the President of the United States to present the Distinguished Flying Cross to Amelia Earhart Putnam: Resolved by the Senate and House of Representatives of the United States of America in Congress assembled, That the President of the United States is authorized to present the Distinguished Flying Cross to Amelia Earhart Putnam for displaying heroic courage and skill as a navigator, at risk of her life, by her nonstop flight in her plane, unnamed, from Harbor Grace, Newfoundland, to Londonderry, Ireland, on May 20, 1932, by which she became the first and only woman, and the second person, to cross the Atlantic Ocean in a plane in solo flight, and also establish new records for speed and elapsed time between the two continents. (Distinguished Flying Cross Society)

Amelia Earhart was no "15 Minutes of Fame" star. She was, and will eternally remain, a universal heroine of enormous stature who blazed more than sky trails. What numbers in her King's Numerology^{tm} chart . . .

- Reveal her independence and courage?
- Reflect her adventurous spirit and daring do?
- Indicate her powerful public persona?
- Suggest her mysterious and tragic disappearance near Howland Island in 1937 (just twenty-two days before her 40th birthday) in her attempt to circumnavigate the globe?

To answer these questions let's look at some of the major aspects and highlights of Earhart's chart.

AMELIA EARHART – CHART HIGHLIGHTS

Basic Matrix: Amelia Mary Earhart

LP	Exp.	PE	Soul	MS	Nature	MN	Voids
11-2	7	99-9	22-4	33-6	3	77-5	6

Name Timeline (NTL): Amelia Mary Earhart			
	First	Middle	Last
Names	Amelia	Mary	Earhart
Timeline	birth to 23	24 to 44	45 to 79
General	23	21	35
IR Set	5	3	8
	7	5	1
Master #s		77	55
		Dies here	

The 11-2 Lifepath

The 11-2 cipher set is the Master Achiever/Aspirant number. It contains enormous potential for action (double 1s) in the realm of relationship (2). Because this 11-2 was in her Lifepath it became the foundation of her life's lessons and work, lessons and work which would gain her global attention.

The 99-9 PE (Performance/Experience, the Role in Life)

One of the prominent numbers in Earhart's Basic Matrix is her PE (Performance/Experience) of 99-9, the number whose symbol is the crown. This is the role she will give on the great life stage. It is the reason for her massive public attention and global recognition.

No number is more universally powerful than the 99-9. As you will recall, Albert Einstein had this powerful master number in his third Grand Pinnacle PE, the core of his Life Matrix. When the 99-9 occurs in a person's Basic Matrix PE position or in a Life Matrix position, it is virtually impossible

Richard Andrew King

for the individual's work or image not to be recognized among the masses. The reason for this is because the number 9 *is* the masses. It contains all numbers within it and, thus, represents all people, regardless of race, creed, color, nationality, language, religion or gender. The number 9 is the *Number of Mankind*. When the 9 is multiplied eleven times to become the master number 99, it manifests great power among the public, the result is almost always universal recognition.

To strengthen this very powerful 99-9 Basic Matrix PE, the Grand/Core Pinnacle of Earhart's 11-2 Lifepath is also a 9 (see Earhart's Life Matrix, following). This is a dynamic connection because the Grand Pinnacle can be likened to the center of her world. Therefore, her performance in life (PE) and the core of her life (Grand Pinnacle) are both 9s. This creates a condition of *stacking*, the simultaneous occurrence of the same number, numbers, or number patterns in a chart.

One major feature of the 9 is that it can be dominant and domineering. It rules all numbers because all numbers are not only contained within it but they are also reflected by it. This energy of dominance is an asset for people who want to win and succeed. Thus, it gives those who want to conquer – whether they are conquering unknown challenges or challengers – a decisive edge. Without question, Amelia Earhart was a conqueror, not simply of air travel but also of people's hearts, minds and imaginations the world over.

The 77-5 Material Nature (MN) & Name Timeline PE of "Mary"

Deep and diverse. This phrase can easily be associated with the 77-5 number grouping. The 5 rules diversity, motion, speed. The 7 rules thought, reflection, withdrawal, privacy, depth. Earhart's Material Nature was a 77-5, thus giving her a reflective, thoughtful manner and personality that loved speed and adventure.

The 77-5 is also the PE associated with her Name Timeline of "Mary" which is reflected in its 3/77-5 IR set (21 of Mary + 56 Specific Lifepath = 77). This would help describe the time period of her tragic and mysterious disappearance when she was 39. The timeline of "Mary" was from ages 24 to 44, which obviously reflected her disappearance and demise. For more on timelines and forecasting methods, read *The King's Book of Numerology II: Forecasting – Part I.*

55-1 Name PE of "Earhart"

When the name "Earhart" mixes energetically with her Lifepath, the number 55 emerges (35 of "Earhart" + 20 Lifepath root = 55). The 55 is the master number of exploration, adventure, experience, motion, speed, movement, freedom, revolution, rebellion, uniqueness, independence, leadership and solo pioneering. When the two 5s are added together, the result is the number 10, which in reduction is a 1 (1 + 0 = 1). The number 1 is the leader, doer, activist, creator, maverick and lone wolf.

The 55-1, therefore, represents the solo pioneer, the revolutionary who sets out to blaze new trails, explore new territories and make a mark. It is an extremely unique energy. Both the 5 and 1 are fire signs, so this 55-1 master energy is full of fire, is nothing but fire . . . wild fire. It is virtually impossible to control the 55-1. It does what it wants to do and cannot be contained. With freedom and leadership as its essence, its mission in life is to lift its arm and wave it forward, bravely declaring, "Follow Me!" Interestingly, all of the individuals featured in this work have the 55-1 master energy strongly situated in their charts. This helps define their unique personalities. To be sure, it reflected the adventurous, pioneering, will, courage, independence and "daring-do" persona of one Amelia Mary Earhart, "Queen of the Skies."

The 1/8 Influence Reality (IR) Set

Amelia Earhart's courage, will to succeed, independence, pioneering spirit and action-oriented persona—qualities of the 1 energy—were a major aspect of who Earhart was. This spirit of independence is also located in her Life Matrix as part of the 1/8 IR set which occupies three of her four Challenges (the 1st, 3rd and 4th Challenges).

This 1/8 IR set indicates the self, ego, pioneer, entrepreneur and yang energy (the 1) manifesting itself in the arena of the number 8, which represents commerce, business, interaction, connection, continuity, engagement, social power, status, acclaim, orchestration and being in-the-loop.

Earhart's life journey certainly represented this 1/8 IR Set. She was a global celebrity icon of her day, worldly renowned and admired. For a correlation of a modern day global icon with the same

Richard Andrew King

1/8 IR set in her chart and in the exact same three Challenge positions (1st, 3rd and 4th) look no further than Oprah Winfrey, the "Queen of Media," who is also featured later in this work.

Think of how socially powerful Oprah is and you'll have some idea of how powerful Amelia Earhart was. In fact, these two icons have many of the same numbers and master numbers in their charts, which one would expect since their life journeys are generally similar. Both women were/are leaders in their fields; both were/are extremely bright, charismatic and independent; both were/are global icons and business women; both were/are pioneers and trend-setters; both were/are admired by the masses. Besides sharing this identical 1/8 IR Challenge pattern in their charts, they also share the master numbers 11, 22, 33, 55 and 77. Additionally, they each have a 7 Expression and a 33-6 Material Soul. Oprah has a 5 Nature and Amelia has a 5 Material Nature.

It is this kind of comparison that will hopefully move you, the reader, closer to the reality between one's personal numbers and destiny. People living similar lives will have similar numbers. Life is not random. Life is structured. Therefore, similar lives will have similar structures. Another pair of historic icons who had similar charts were Marilyn Monroe and Princess Diana. Both were famous beyond belief; both had difficult childhoods and both died tragic deaths. They, too, are featured in this work.

The point of all this is to show the truth of numerology through people's lives. Numbers are a fact of our existence and the more we study life and numbers with an open, clear, unbiased, truth-seeking mind, we cannot help but subscribe to the reality that destiny is clearly revealed in numbers.

AMELIA EARHART & OPRAH WINFREY: BASIC MATRIX GRIDS

Since we've been talking about Amelia's and Oprah's numbers, let's compare their Basic Matrices. Although specifically different, they are generally similar. Notice they both have 11-2, 22-4, 33-6, 5, 7 and 9 in their Basic Matrices. Reducing the master numbers to single numbers or *crowns*, we see the numerical similarities in a more simple fashion: 2-4-5-6-7-9. Earhart has a 3 in her Nature but that's the only differing number in this aspect of their charts.

Basic Matrix: Amelia Mary Earhart

LP	Exp.	PE	Soul	MS	Nature	MN	Voids
11-2	7	99-9	22-4	33-6	3	77-5	6

Basic Matrix: Oprah Gail Winfrey

LP	Exp.	PE	Soul	MS	Nature	MN	Voids
22-4	7	11-2	11-2	33-6	5	9	2 & 4

MASTER NUMBERS IN AMELIA EARHART'S NUMEROLOGY CHART

As we learned in discussing Albert Einstein's chart, master numbers are a major player in those individuals who are generally recognized as being in the famous icon category. Master numbers, as has been said, are like nuclear energy. They are powerful, and their presence creates powerful lives.

The following chart reveals the master numbers appearing in Amelia Earhart's full numerology chart. The only two master numbers missing are the master number 44 and the master number 66. (next page)

Richard Andrew King

Master Numbers in Amelia Earhart's Chart	
11	Lifepath 1st Pinnacle PE 4th Pinnacle (Crown) PE
22	Soul 1st Epoch PE
33	Material Soul 1st Challenge PE
44	none
55	Name Timeline PE of "Earhart"
66	none
77	Material Nature Name Timeline PE of "Mary"
88	2nd Challenge PE
99	Life PE-Performance/Experience (Role of Life)

AMELIA EARHART: LIFE MATRIX

Following is the Life Matrix of Amelia Earhart. Notice the 1/8 IR sets in her Challenges; her 9 Grand Pinnacle and master numbers.

LIFE MATRIX
Void: 6
AMELIA MARY EARHART
24 JULY 1897

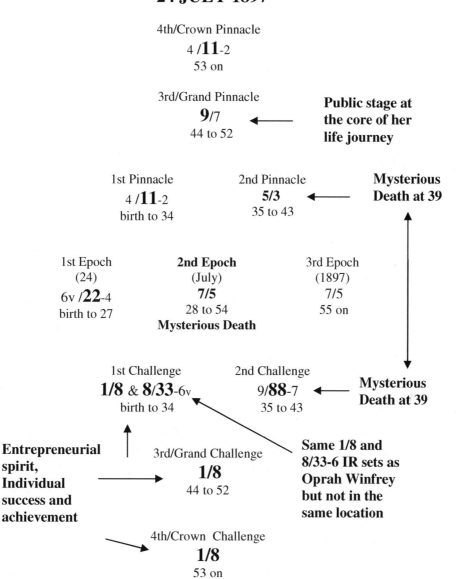

4th/Crown Pinnacle
4 /**11**-2
53 on

3rd/Grand Pinnacle
9/7
44 to 52

**Public stage at
the core of her
life journey**

1st Pinnacle
4 /**11**-2
birth to 34

2nd Pinnacle
5/3
35 to 43

**Mysterious
Death at 39**

1st Epoch
(24)
6v /**22**-4
birth to 27

2nd Epoch
(July)
7/5
28 to 54
Mysterious Death

3rd Epoch
(1897)
7/5
55 on

1st Challenge
1/8 & **8/33**-6v
birth to 34

2nd Challenge
9/**88**-7
35 to 43

**Mysterious
Death at 39**

**Entrepreneurial
spirit,
Individual
success and
achievement**

3rd/Grand Challenge
1/8
44 to 52

**Same 1/8 and
8/33-6 IR sets as
Oprah Winfrey
but not in the
same location**

4th/Crown Challenge
1/8
53 on

Richard Andrew King

MYSTERIOUS DISAPPEARANCE AND DEATH

The tragic deaths of iconic individuals such as Amelia Earhart, Marilyn Monroe, Princess Diana, John F. Kennedy, Elvis Presley and Michael Jackson certainly generate a sense of sorrowful loss and public interest. However, to have also died not just under mysterious circumstances but in unknown and unresolved circumstances is a Shakespearian formula for endless fascination and inquisitive speculation.

Master aviatrix Amelia Earhart and her world-class navigator, Fred Noonan, disappeared on Friday, 2 July 1937 in the Pacific Ocean en route to Howland Island (a 55-1 Expression matching the Name Timeline PE of "Earhart!"), approximately 1700 nautical miles southwest of Honolulu, Hawaii. The search for Earhart and Noonan was the most costly and intensive air and sea search by the United States Navy and Coast Guard up to that time. After the U.S. ceased its search, Earhart's husband, American publisher, promoter and author, George Putnam, mounted his own search but it, too, was unsuccessful.

The mystery surrounding the demise of Amelia Earhart is revealed in her King's Numerology[tm] chart through a rather unfortunate grouping of numbers.

The number most associated with mystery, secrecy, trouble and turmoil is the number 7. The number most associated with loss and accidents is the number 5. The number most associated with endings is the 9. The number signifying tension and relationship conflict is the 2.

The following grid shows the numbers and numerical patterns surrounding Earhart at the time of her disappearance. Together, the amalgam of these numbers: 2-5-7-9 created a condition capable of generating a tragic scenario like the one Earhart unfortunately endured.

NUMBER PATTERNS OF TRAGEDY

Some of the components in the following grid have not been discussed nor need to be at this point. It would just complicate things. However, of note is the extreme amount of 2-5-7-9 energy in total which indicates an overwhelming amount of simultaneous loss, suffering and endings. All of these numeric energies were *stacked* on the day of Amelia Earhart's disappearance — 2 July 1937. Hauntingly, the name *Howland Island* and the *Earhart* Name Timeline PE (the *outcome* of Earhart) are both a 55-1, as mentioned earlier. What are the odds? How much more precise can destiny be? Astounding!

Amelia Earhart's Numbers on the day of her Disappearance

Life Expression and PE	**7/9**
Timeline of *Mary* (ages 24 to 44)	**3/77-5**
Letter Timeline "Y" of *Mary* (ages 38 to 44)	**7/9**
2nd Pinnacle	**5/3**
2nd Challenge	**9/7**
2nd Epoch	**7/5**
Calendar Year (1937)	**2/9**
Calendar Year, Personal Cycle Month	**5/3**
Age Timeline Universal Month	**9/7**
Personal Year Universal Month	**2/9**
Day of Disappearance (2 July 1937)	**2/9**
Day of Disappearance Pinnacle (2 July 1937)	**9/7**
Day of Disappearance: Universal Date (2 July 1937)	**2/9**

Richard Andrew King

SUMMARY

Amelia Earhart was a rock star of her day and her numbers prove it, just as Albert Einstein's numbers reflected his immense fame and fortune. Following are a few major highlights of Earhart's life and numbers.

- Her 99-9 Life PE and 9 Grand Pinnacle reveal massive public appeal and universal recognition.
- Her 55-1 Name Timeline PE of "Earhart" reflects her extreme individuality and revolutionary spirit—doing things other people would not or could not do.
- The haunting "coincidence" that the name "Howland Island" is also a 55-1 is really no coincidence at all but one major numerical thread in the mosaic of Earhart's dramatic life, disappearance and destiny.
- Her 1/8 IR set in her 1st, 3rd (Grand) and 4th (Crown) Challenges reveal her entrepreneurial spirit, commercialism and interaction with success and worldly fortune.
- The enormous *stacking* of the numbers 2-5-7-9 on the day of Amelia Earhart's mysterious and tragic disappearance and ultimate demise reveal the tensions, conflicts, accident, loss, chaos, turmoil, suffering, tragedy and endings associated with the event—arguably the most famous mysterious disappearance in modern world history.
- The general amount of master numbers in her chart is significant, the only two being absent are the 44 and 66.

Truly, Amelia Mary Earhart was a world-class icon and global phenom, a powerful person whose magnetic, charismatic and universal persona will reverberate eternally through the historic halls of the rich and famous.

AMELIA EARHART – QUOTES

Adventure is worthwhile in itself.

The most effective way to do it, is to do it.

Courage is the price that life exacts for granting peace.

Never interrupt someone doing what you said couldn't be done.

The woman who can create her own job is the woman who will win fame and fortune.

Women must try to do things as men have tried. When they fail, their failure must be a challenge to others.

Worry retards reaction and makes clear-cut decisions impossible.

The most difficult thing is the decision to act, the rest is merely tenacity.

[Women] must pay for everything . . . They do get more glory than men for comparable feats. But, also, women get more notoriety when they crash.

Richard Andrew King

HISTORIC ICON #3

E L V I S   P R E S L E Y

Born: Elvis Aaron Presley – 8 January 1935
Died – 16 August 1977, age 42

----

* King of Rock and Roll

Before Elvis, there was nothing. ~ John Lennon
Elvis was the king. No doubt about it. ~ Rod Stewart
Elvis is the greatest cultural force in the Twentieth Century.
~ Leonard Bernstein

(Photo courtesy of Wikimedia Commons)

Richard Andrew King

Few entertainers have captured the imagination of the world more than Elvis Aaron Presley, born on 8 January 1935, passing from this life on 16 August 1977 at the age of forty-two. Decades after his death, The King of Rock 'n' Roll still fascinates people the world over, magnetizing them to his life and persona. Some questions . . .

- What numbers made Elvis a global icon?
- Why was he such a great singer and performer?
- What is special and rare about his Basic Matrix?
- Why couldn't he remain married to Priscilla?
- What is significant about his numbers the month he died?
- How was his destiny tied to Colonel Parker and Sun Records?

There are no accidents in the universe. We all have our destinies and the King of Rock 'n' Roll had his in spades. The first indication of Elvis Presley's extreme popularity is revealed in his Basic Matrix.

Basic Matrix: Elvis Aaron Presley

LP	Exp.	PE	Soul	MS	Nature	MN	Voids
9	9	99-9	66-3	66-3	6	33-6	2 & 8

In the King's Numerology™ the numbers 3-6-9 form the *Artistic Triad*. No three-ciphered combination reflects more artistry, communication, self-expression, love, harmony and universal appeal than these three numbers. Although not an uncommon triumvirate, what is extremely rare is that Elvis's Artistic Triad is composed of all master numbers: 33-66-99! Therefore, these master numbers can be defined as the *Master Artistic Triad*, a most unique combination, especially when appearing in the Basic Matrix.

ELVIS PRESLEY'S MASTER ARTISTIC TRIAD

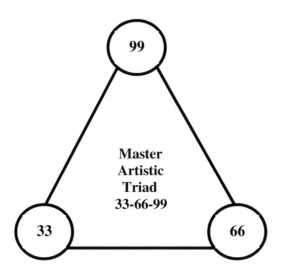

The most significant aspect of this configuration is that the 99—the most powerful public and universal master number—occupies Presley's life PE, the ultimate role of his life. Where have we seen this 99 PE before? If you answered in the chart of Amelia Earhart, you are right. Just as Earhart was *Queen of the Skies*, Elvis Presley was the *King of Rock 'n' Roll.* As we will also remember, the Grand Pinnacle PE (the core of one's Lifepath) of Albert Einstein was also a 99! With all of his accolades, Einstein could be called the *King of 20th Century Science.*

The symbol for the number 9 is the crown. When the 9 is multiplied eleven times to become the 99 master number, its power magnifies to an extremely high level of notoriety. Thus, the 99 is the *Master's Master*, which can be ciphered as 99-9 as we've previously discussed. In the case of Presley, Earhart and Einstein it garners the title of universal royalty.

Interestingly, Presley's 99 lifetime PE is not the only 99 in his chart. His Crown Epoch PE from the year of his birth (1935) is also a 99! Furthermore, the sum of his three Name Timeline PEs is also a 99! Obviously, it is no accident that Elvis Aaron Presley was, and continues to be, a potent force in the world of historic icons because of his numbers.

Richard Andrew King

Name Timeline PEs of Elvis Presley

22 (Elvis PE) + **22** (Aaron PE) + **55** (Presley PE) = **99**

Name Timeline (NTL): Elvis Aaron Presley			
	First	Middle	Last
Names	Elvis	Aaron	Presley
Timeline	birth to 22	23 to 44	45 to 81
General	22	22	37
IR Set	4	4	1
	4	4	1
Master #s	22	22	55

Obviously, this 99 triad of Presley's derived from his lifetime PE, 3rd Epoch PE and Name Timeline PEs generates a tristack of the most publicly powerful master number there is. It is this 99 tristack that was a major ingredient in creating the global icon of Elvis as the *King of Rock 'n' Roll*. No other featured icon in this work has a 99-9 Triumvirate. It is unadulterated power in spades!

OTHER MASTER NUMBERS IN ELVIS PRESLEY'S LIFE

The 99 is certainly not the only powerful master number in Elvis' life, as we have already seen to some degree. In fact, Presley had a slew of master numbers in his chart. The only two not present are the 11 and 77. His Basic Matrix houses the 33 in his Material Nature, as well as the 66 in both his Soul and Material Soul. In fact, the 66 in these positions was the number playing a major role in Presley's great voice and love of communication. The 33 in his Material Nature contributed mightily to his loving and generous personality, which has been commented upon by many people who knew him well. In fact, one almost never hears any negative comments about Elvis. He was, indeed, a truly beloved human being. In the words of another American icon, Frank Sinatra said of Elvis, *He was a warm, considerate and generous man.*

Master Numbers in Elvis Presley's Chart	
11	none
22	"Elvis"
	Name Timeline PE of "Elvis"
	"V" of "Elvis" ("V" is the 22nd letter of the alphabet)
	Letter Timeline PE of the "V" in "Elvis"
	"Aaron"
	Name Timeline PE of "Aaron"
	4th House of work, structure, stability, security
33	Material Nature
44	"Elvis Aaron"
	4th (Crown) Pinnacle PE
55	Name Timeline PE of "Presley"
66	Soul
	Material Soul
77	none
88	1st Challenge PE
99	Life PE-Performance/Experience (Role of Life)
	3rd (Crown) Epoch PE
	The sum of the Name Timeline PEs:
	22 (Elvis PE) + 22 (Aaron PE) + 55 (Presley PE) = 99

The 22 Master Number

In looking at these master numbers in Presley's chart, it is impossible to miss the large amount of 22 *master builder* energy and there is an inordinate amount of it in his chart – a whopping hepstack (seven stack) of this exemplary binary representing power and wealth. Perhaps the manifestation of the 22 master number in his life is what motivated Presley to say, *I have no use for bodyguards, but I have very specific use for two highly trained certified public accountants.*

The 33 Master Number

The 33 is, arguably, the most dynamic master number reflecting pleasure, image, artistic self-expression, beauty, sex and communication of all types—vocal, visual, literary, personal. It is so powerful, in fact, in can be labeled as the "Opiate of Pleasure." Although it can be expressed positively, as in the charts of Helen Keller, Martin Luther King, Winston Churchill, Mother Teresa, General George Patton and others, its unchecked negative energies have, arguably, been responsible for destroying more reputations, characters, careers and souls than any other master number. The 33's pleasure energies are highly addictive, especially reflected in the areas of partying, sex and drugs.

It is no secret that Elvis was addicted to drugs, which led to his demise. Yet, a plethora of other famous celebrities have also fallen prey to the pejorative pleasure potency of the master number 33. Charlie Sheen, Lindsay Lohan, Whitney Houston, Phil Spector, Tiger Woods, Amy Winehouse, Marilyn Monroe, Michael Jackson and Anna Nicole Smith, just to name a few. Wyatt Earp and General George Armstrong Custer also were magnetized to the 33's power of self-image.

The 44 Master Number

Besides his trademark voice, another personal trademark of Elvis Presley was his T.C.B. acronym which stands for "Taking Care of Business." This motto was a powerful part of his life. It touched every aspect of his life from his music, to his jewelry, clothing, vehicles and personal belongings. The addcap of the 44 master number is 8 (4 + 4 = 8), the number of business and commerce. The 44 is associated by the structural aspect of the 8, maintaining a sense of organization and work ethic.

This powerful master number played a significant role in Presley's life. It occupies the PE position of his Crown Pinnacle (see his Life Matrix). It is also the number associated with his first two names, "Elvis Presley," both of which are a 22, thus creating the 44 (22 + 22 = 44). Here we see yet another powerful master energy combination in his life.

The 55 Master Number

The master number 55 houses a 1 crown. The Name Timeline PE of "Presley" is a 55, which can be written as 55-1 (5 + 5 = 10: 1 + 0 = 1). The 55-1 represents the most unique and independent energy of all the master numbers. Anyone with a 55 in his or her chart will be a one-of-a-kind individual. In many ways such an individual will be a revolutionary, visionary, pioneer, trend-setter, maverick and rebel. 55-1 people are difficult to control because they are their own people. The numbers 1 and 5 are both fire signs. The 1 is ego-centric, extremely independent and strong willed; the 5 is totally freedom-oriented, unconventional, mercurial, diverse, exploratory. These two numbers, the 1 and 5, therefore are extremely active and dynamic. Every individual in this book has a 55-1 in their King's Numerology[tm] natal chart except Marilyn Monroe, whose 55-1 appears in the Material Nature of her common name rather than her birth name.

A few other historic and iconic individuals having the 55-1 master number in their charts are listed below. As history will corroborate, each of them has a legacy of being truly unique and individualistic.

Richard Andrew King

Sampling of Individuals with 55-1 in Their Charts

- Albert Schweitzer—humanitarian & Nobel Laureate

- Apolo Ohno—speed skater

- Bill Gates—computer entrepreneur

- Bill Walsh—football coach & revolutionary

- Dick Button—ice skater

- Douglas MacArthur—general

- Evan Lysacek—ice skater

- George Washington—general & 1st U.S. President

- Kim Yu-Na—ice skater

- King Arthur—mythical king

- Neil Armstrong—astronaut (1st man on the moon)

- William Shakespeare—dramatist

- William Wallace—revolutionary patriot

The 66 Master Number

A master sibling to the 33 is the 66. Each of these master numbers has the other's root number as its crown—the 33 has the 6 and the 66 has the 3. Both are extremely powerful creatively, artistically, communicatively. The difference is that the 33 creates love (6) through massive self-expression (33) while the 66 creates massive self-expression (3) through love (66).

It is the double 66 in Elvis' Soul and Material Soul that gave him a desire to create beautiful, harmonious, melodious and resonant vocal tones and music. In other words, his legendary voice was rooted in love. Arguably, no other singer in history has had as many impersonators as the King of Rock and Roll. Such was the power of his voice. Certainly this double 66 played a major role in his fame, fortune and legacy.

The 88 Master Number

No master number exudes the potential for spirituality more than the 88, whose crown is a 7. Oftentimes, however, spirituality comes through trial, suffering and hardship—traits common to Presley's childhood. The master number 88 is located in Elvis' 1st Challenge, the early part of his life. It was here that he also acquired a great connection with gospel music that remained with him throughout his life.

This 88-7 ($8 + 8 = 16: 1 + 6 = 7$) period reflected a shy Elvis. The number 7 is reclusive. It was during his maturation years that Elvis was told by more than one person that he couldn't sing and would never make it as a singer! How many times has such a story been told—that someone could never "make it" who ultimately turned out to be successful beyond imagination?

Richard Andrew King

LIFE MATRIX
Voids: 2 & 8
ELVIS AARON PRESLEY
8 JANUARY 1935

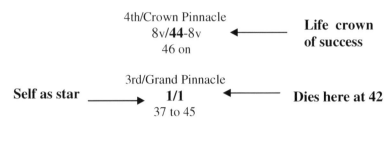

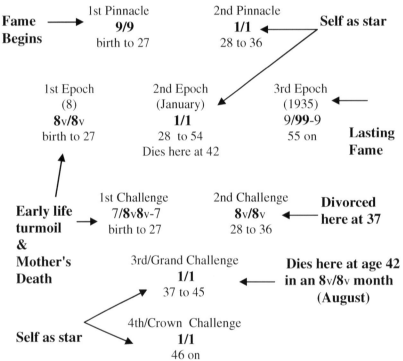

Beyond the master numbers in his Life Matrix, one of the number combinations that stands out is the 1/1 IR set; fuller ciphering is 1/(9)/1. The number 1 rules the self, ego, star, yang energy, individuality, independence, action. Although Elvis has a great deal of 9 energy in his chart—the energy of the public stage and universal appeal—this 1/1 cipher set dominates his Life Matrix, occupying his Grand Pinnacle, Grand Challenge (the core of his 9 Lifepath), 2nd Pinnacle, 2nd

Epoch and Crown Challenge. With all this 1/(9)/1 energy, it was impossible for him not to be the center of his 9-dominated life in a very big way.

Upon further observation, we see that the only IR sets in his Life Matrix are 1/1, 7/7, 8/8 and 9/9. This combination speaks to individuality (1), isolation (7), business (8) and the public arena (9). There is no 6 energy of the home and family in his life's journey, as illustrated by the Life Matrix, even though he did have 6 energy in his Basic Matrix (personal profile). Desires aside, this 1-7-8-9 energy grouping in his Life Matrix made Elvis both a public and private man but not a family man per se. Basically, he had a very public life (9) in which he and his talents were the center of attention, the star (1).

THE 2 AND 8 VOIDS

Elvis had no 2s or 8s in his birth name. The number 2 is derived from the letters B-K-T and the number 8 originates from H-Q-Z. The 2 is the first of the social numbers 2-4-6-8 and governs close personal relationships. The 8 is the highest octave of the social numbers and rules social interaction and business.

With this combination of the 2 and 8 void, especially in conjunction with the plethora of 1 and 9 energy in his chart, it would have been very difficult for Elvis to have had any really close and enduring family relationships. He was a man for the masses; not a man for a family. This is one reason his marriage to Priscilla failed. It's not that he didn't want it; it's that his numbers neither allowed nor supported it.

As we see in his Life Matrix, his 1st Epoch and his 2nd Challenge both manifested and 8v/8v IR set (the 'v' stands for void). This 8v/8v pattern brings disconnections in life. It was during his 1st Epoch that he lost his mother with whom he was very close. It was during his 2nd Challenge that his marriage to Priscilla ended in divorce. *Togetherness* is challenging with an 8 void.

Presley's 1st Challenge was, in simple terms, a 7/(9)/7. However, the outcome 7 (the one on the right side of the slash) houses an 88 master root. Because Presley had an 8 void in his chart, this 88 outcome can be further written as 88v, thus making the entire IR set a 7/(9)/88v-16-7. The number seven always creates spiritual testing, turmoil, suffering and potential chaos. With the 8s being voided, this compounded the turmoil issues and was a clear indication there would be painful disconnections in his early life, which history has proven.

The numbers of Presley's destiny forced him to be a star on the public stage and to suffer the loses he did experience. As 20th Century Saint Charan Singh states,

> *All men come into this world with a destiny of their own which goes on pushing them relentlessly on the course already marked out for them.*

In a numerology sense, it is our numbers that define our destiny, and it is destiny which pushes each of us relentlessly on the course already marked out for us. Elvis' life was no different. The 1s, 7s, 8s and 9s in his chart are the labels showing the destiny driving him to stardom . . . and in many ways to heartbreak and destruction, which we'll discuss after a brief look at two of the constants in his life—his manager, Colonel Parker, and his music labels, Sun Records and RCA Victor.

COLONEL PARKER, SUN RECORDS & RCA VICTOR

Nothing is coincidental in this universe. Everything has a cause. We've discussed the importance of the number 1 in Elvis' life, especially in his Life Matrix, but there's more.

The name "Presley" is a 1 in reduction. Interestingly, Elvis' long-time manager, Tom Parker, was commonly known as Colonel Parker. The name *Colonel Parker* is also a 1 in reduction! Not only that, but the name of his first music label *Sun Records* is a 1, as well as *RCA Victor* who purchased Presley's contract from Sun Records! Therefore, three of the most crucial aspects of his career—his manager and both music labels—had numbers matching the 1s in his chart. Is this coincidental or destiny revealed through numbers?

THE DEMISE OF ELVIS PRESLEY

Elvis Presley's life, although positively powerful in many aspects, also had its dark side, as is well known. His prescription drug abuse has been linked to his death. Do his numbers show this aspect of his life? Yes. Let's take a look.

Master numbers are powerful but, as has been mentioned, they are like nuclear energy—enormously positive but equally negative. The master numbers 33 and 66 are pleasure-oriented energies, aka Pleasure Based Opiates (PBOs). These are strongly aspected in Presley's chart. In one way or another, they played a part in his tragic demise, coupled with the 2 and 8 voids.

It is not uncommon that people who have weight issues often have the number 8 in their charts. The 8 governs flow and management and Presley obviously had a difficult time managing some aspects of his personal life. How tragic and sad it was for those of us who grew up in the same generation to see Elvis, the King, deteriorate in his later years.

With the 8 being voided in his chart, this was certainly problematic. With all the pleasure energy created by the master numbers 33 and 66 juxtaposed in a Life Matrix with a strong 8 void, this spelled trouble. Was it the only cause of his problems? Of course not, but it was definitely a factor. Regardless of how stable a person is, fame and fortune always create pressures of enormous magnitude. Are human beings capable of managing all the pressures of constantly being in the public spotlight? It's not normal, and there is a lot to be said for normalcy. As Shakespeare said, *Uneasy lies the head that wears a crown*, and the crown of public worship and being labeled as the *King of Rock 'n Roll* or simply, *The King*, had to have had an effect of uneasy magnitude . . . and temptation . . . for Presley.

ELVIS PRESLEY – NUMBERS AT DEATH

Stacking of the Number 5

The numbers appearing in the chart of Elvis Presley during the month of his death are telling and involve the principle of *stacking*—the simultaneous occurrence of the same number or number patterns in a chart. We've seen the result of stacking in the disappearance of Amelia Earhart and it is also apparent in Presley's chart, although the numbers of his death do not hold the mystery and intrigue that Earhart's did. The following chart shows the number patterns during the month of Elvis Presley's passing (concepts are taught in *The King's Book of Numerology II: Forecasting - Part I*). Without being overly technical, the important aspect is the amount of *stacking* involved in the number 5. What the chart reveals is not a mistake. It's pretty amazing, isn't it?

Elvis Presley's Month of Death
14 Stack of 5 energy!
16 August 1977
Dies in the Letter Timeline "N" of "Aaron"

Dies in the "N" Letter Timeline of "Aaron"	5
Dies in the "N" Letter Timeline PE of "Aaron"	5
Age Timeline Cycle Month	5
Age Timeline Cycle Month PE	5
Age Timeline Universal Month	5
Age Timeline Universal Month PE	5
Calendar Year Timeline Cycle Month	5
Calendar Year Timeline Cycle Month PE	5
Calendar Year Timeline Universal Month	5
Calendar Year Timeline Universal Month PE	5
Personal Year Timeline Cycle Month	5
Personal Year Timeline Cycle Month PE	5
Personal Year Timeline Universal Month	5
Personal Year Timeline Universal Month PE	5

This grid contains a 14 stack of 5 energy! The 14 also reduces to a 5 as well. The number 5, a fire sign in numerology, represents attributes of detachment, loss, change and the five senses. This is an enormous amount of energy, and Presley's life and numbers certainly reflect massive loss in the month of his death. As a note, this kind of almost overbearing stacking of 5 energy was also present in the chart of The United States on 11 September 2001 (aka 9/11), a day that changed the world forever. It would seem that both towers and kings are subject to mighty falls when the 5 is stacked appreciably.

The 8v/8v Disconnect

Yet, there's more critical numerical information regarding Elvis' disconnection from life and that involves the 8v/8v IR tristack. We've seen that his mother died in his 1st Epoch of 8v/8v; his divorce from Priscilla was in his 2nd Challenge of 8v/8v. His Crown (4th) Pinnacle is an 8v/8v. Obviously, this 8v/8v IR tristack generated problems for Elvis because with both the Influence and Reality numbers being an 8, an 8 void sixstack was created.

Adding to the explanation of the 8 void creating losses, Presley died in August, the 8th calendar month which, when added to his 9 Expression, would have created an 8v/8v energy pattern for that month. Interestingly, August of 1977 for Elvis was the 512 month of his life, another 8 in reduction (5 + 1 + 2 = 8). When his 9 Expression is added to this 8, the outcome is 8 (8 + 9 = 17: 1 + 7 = 8). Adjusting for his 8 void, the IR set of his *Lifetime Monthly Timeline* or LMT (the actual months of a person's life) is also an 8v/8v. All of these combinations create a *decaset* (10 set) of 8 void energy—the sixstack in his Life Matrix, the calendar month of August (8v/8v) and the 512 months he was alive (8v/8v)!

Combined with the enormous amount of 5 stacking, the energies present during the month of his death revealed intense loss and disconnection, obviously resulting in Presley's death.

Richard Andrew King

SUMMARY

John Lennon couldn't have said it better, *Before Elvis, there was nothing.* Rod Stewart's comment is no less reverential, *Elvis was the king. No doubt about it.* Leonard Bernstein's observance that *Elvis is the greatest cultural force in the Twentieth Century* only added to the astronomical adulation to an artist and a man who changed the world of music forever. Decades after his passing, Elvis Presley is still a giant among giants in the entertainment industry. There was no one like him before and there has been no one like him since. He was truly *the King.*

HIGHLIGHTS OF ELVIS PRESLEY'S LIFE

Here are a few of the major numerological aspects of Elvis Presley's life of fame and fortune.

- The 33-66-99 *Master Artistic Triad* in his Basic Matrix
- The triad of 9s in his Umbrella (Lifepath, Expression and PE)
- The 99-9 tristack in his PE, 3rd Epoch PE and Name Timeline PEs
- The hepstack (seven stack) of 22 master builder energy in his chart
- The double 66 in his Soul and Material Soul
- The 8v/8v disconnecting IR set occurring at the most troublesome times in his life—his early years (1st Epoch) of family turmoil and the death of his beloved mother, his 2nd Challenge where he and Priscilla divorced, and the month of his death.
- The quintstack of 1/1 energy within his Life Matrix—the framework of his 9 Lifepath (creates a decaset of 1 energy)
- The 14 stack of 5 energy in the month of his death
- The decaset of 8 voided energy in his chart

It is hoped that this short numerical assessment of Elvis Presley's life has further helped to reveal the relationship between the numbers associated with a person's natal data (full name at birth and birth date) and his life. Powerful numbers reveal powerful destinies. This is certainly no more obvious than in the life of Elvis Aaron Presley, the King of Rock 'n Roll, whose powerful numbers created a powerful life and universal legacy of what it is to be an historic icon simply known as, the King.

(Photo courtesy of Wikimedia Commons)

ELVIS PRESLEY – QUOTES

Whatever I will become will be what God has chosen for me.

I believe in the Bible. I believe that all good things come from God. I don't believe I'd sing the way I do if God hadn't wanted me to.

From the time I was a kid, I always knew something was going to happen to me. Didn't know exactly what.

When I was a child I was a dreamer. I read comic books, and I was the hero of the comic book. I saw movies, and I was the hero in the movie. So every dream I have ever dreamed has come true a thousand times.

I have no use for bodyguards, but I have very specific use for two highly trained certified public accountants.

The Lord can give and the Lord can take away. I might be herding sheep next year.

Richard Andrew King

More than anything else, I want the folks back at home to think right of me.

There are too many people that depend on me. I'm too obligated. I'm in too far to get out.

HISTORIC ICON #4

GENERAL GEORGE PATTON

Born: George Smith Patton, Jr. – 11 November 1885

Died – 21 December 1945, age 60

* General, Army of the United States: 14 April 1945

* U.S. Military Academy at West Point: 1909

* U.S. Army *Master of the Sword*

* Old Blood and Guts

(Photo courtesy of Wikimedia Commons)

George Patton was the most brilliant commander of an army in

the open field that our or any other service produced.

~ General Dwight D. Eisenhower

[*Patton: A Genius for War* Carlo D'Este]

Richard Andrew King

PATTON. The name is legend. The man is George Smith Patton, Jr., arguably the most memorable American military hero of World War II and perhaps of the 20th Century. "Old Blood and Guts" as he was known, was a brilliant, eccentric, enigmatic, flamboyant, arrogant, war-loving, larger-than-life iconic leader whose demeanor, presence and words could inspire ordinary men to win extraordinary battles. Without question, George Patton was a one-of-a-kind swashbuckling superstar built for war and with a destiny that supplied it.

Donning flashy ivory-handled nickel-plated revolvers, fire-flamed rhetoric, over-sized stars and an ego to match, Patton was an imposing presence, especially on the battlefield. An avid reader and devout student of war who believed in reincarnation, Old Blood and Guts was born to excel in war and die, ironically and allegedly, as a result of a freak post war vehicle accident.

PROVOCATIVE QUESTIONS

- What number in Patton's chart helped make him a great general?

- What master number gave him his flamboyance and distinctiveness?

- Which lifetime number pattern reflected his 'war management' path?

- What master number reflected his powerful communication skills?

- Which two numbers helped generate his arrogance and dominance?

- What missing number nearly cost him his military career?

THE DESTINY NUMBER OF GENERALSHIP

George Patton's Basic Matrix clearly shows a life of generalship. Notice the 44-8 Lifepath in the following Basic Matrix? This is the numerical vibration most associated with executive management and command. Anyone with a 44-8 LP will be involved with organization, execution, orchestration, management and administration because through the 44 energy the qualities of the 4 (order, organization, service, duty, structure, discipline, stability) rise to the interactive, connective, managerial and executive level of the 8.

Basic Matrix: George Smith Patton Jr.

LP	Exp.	PE	Soul	MS	Nature	MN	Voids
44-8	6	5	5	4	1	9	3

As well as having the 44-8 in his Lifepath, Patton's Letter Timeline (LTL) expressed this master number in the PE of the "R" in his first name, "George," creating an 18-9/44-8 IR set (the 18 is a 9 in reduction and the 44 is an 8 in reduction). This time of his life was from ages 19 to 27. This IR Set of 18-9/44-8 energy is computed by adding the Specific value of the letter "R" which is 18, to his General Lifepath root of 26 to create a 44. The simple IR set is a 9/8. The Specific IR set is, as we see, an 18-9/44-8. It was during this nine year period in which Patton graduated from the United States Military Academy at West Point and also competed in the 1912 Summer Olympics in Stockholm, Sweden, finishing fifth in the first ever modern pentathlon [Wikipedia]. This 18-9/44-8 Letter Timeline (LTL) added to Patton's 44-8 Lifepath creates a double stack of the 44 *generalship* energy.

There is another nuance relating to the 18-9/44-8 Letter Timeline "R." It is contained within the 11-2 master achiever PE energy of "George" whose IR set is 3/11-2. These combined energies of the 11-2 and 44-8 certainly assisted him in his achievements during the ages of 19 to 27 and, as we shall see later, reinforced his generalship "war management" energies reflected in an 11-2/8 IR set dominating his life (see Life Matrix).

The 44-8 is additionally situated in Patton's Letter Timeline in the "R" of his "Jr." suffix, creating another 9/44-8 IR set. Of course he never lived long enough to pass through this last 44-8 LTL period, but nonetheless its energy was an aspect of his life and destiny.

Was the 44-8 master number enough to make Patton a great general? No. It certainly helped make him successful as a strong leader, manager and athlete, but a 44-8 Lifepath is not uncommon, although the Letter Timeline 44-8 PEs are quite rare. What is uncommon as far as Patton's overall success is concerned are other factors in his chart, especially master numbers.

Richard Andrew King

PATTON'S MASTER NUMBERS

Patton had the 11, 22, 33, 44, 55 and 77 master numbers in his life blueprint. This is quite noteworthy. However, what is more noteworthy is the type and placement of specific master numbers in his King's Numerology^{tm} chart.

Every one of the Epochs, Pinnacles and Challenges in Patton's Life Matrix contains a master number except his 1st Challenge, which had no number because he was born on the 11th of November (11 minus 11 = 0). Each of his Name Timeline PEs (*George-Smith-Patton*) houses a master number except the PE of "Jr." *George* carries an 11-2 PE; *Smith* carries a 77-5; *Patton* carries a 22-4. This is a meaningful master number grouping because of its emphasis on the intense interaction with others (11-2), mental depth and alacrity (77-5) and master control through strength and structure (22-4).

Master Numbers in General George S. Patton's Chart	
11	Hexstack (six stack), creating *life linkage* (1st and 2nd Epoch; 2nd, 3rd, 4th Challenges) in addition to his Name Timeline PE of "George" from birth to age 39
22	1st Pinnacle
	3rd Epoch
	Name Timeline PE of Patton from age 64 to 86
33	Crown Pinnacle
	2nd Pinnacle
44	Lifepath
	Letter Timeline PE ("R" of "George" from 19 to 27)
	Letter Timeline PE ("R" of "Jr." from 88 to 96)
55	Grand Pinnacle
66	none
77	Name Timeline PE of "Smith" from age 40 to 63
88	none
99	none

Richard Andrew King

LIFE MATRIX
Void: 3
GEORGE SMITH PATTON JR.
11 NOVEMBER 1885

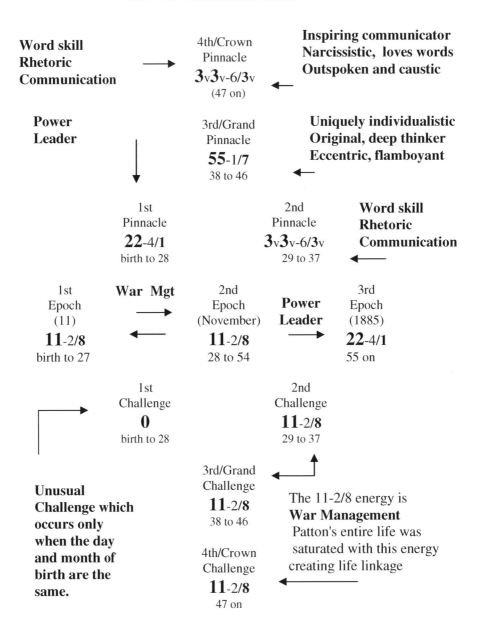

Word skill
Rhetoric
Communication

→

4th/Crown
Pinnacle
3v**3**v-6/**3**v
(47 on)

Inspiring communicator
Narcissistic, loves words
Outspoken and caustic

←

Power
Leader

3rd/Grand
Pinnacle
55-1/7
38 to 46

Uniquely individualistic
Original, deep thinker
Eccentric, flamboyant

←

↓

1st
Pinnacle
22-4/1
birth to 28

2nd
Pinnacle
3v**3**v-6/**3**v
29 to 37

Word skill
Rhetoric
Communication

←

1st
Epoch
(11)
11-2/8
birth to 27

War Mgt
→
←

2nd
Epoch
(November)
11-2/8
28 to 54

Power
Leader
→

3rd
Epoch
(1885)
22-4/1
55 on

1st
Challenge
0
birth to 28

2nd
Challenge
11-2/8
29 to 37

→

Unusual
Challenge which
occurs only
when the day
and month of
birth are the
same.

3rd/Grand
Challenge
11-2/8
38 to 46

↑
←

4th/Crown
Challenge
11-2/8
47 on

←

The 11-2/8 energy is
War Management
Patton's entire life was
saturated with this energy
creating life linkage

Name Timeline (NTL): George Smith Patton, Jr.				
	First	Middle #1	Last	Suffix
Names	George	Smith	Patton	Jr.
Timeline	birth to 39	40 to 63	64 to 86	87 to 96
General	39	24	23	10
IR Set	3	6	5	1
	2	5	4	9
Master #s	11	77	22	

As discussed earlier, *linkage*—the continuous occurrence of the same number, numbers, or number patterns in a chart—is a significant aspect in the destiny of an individual. *Life Linkage* occurs when the same pattern or patterns occur from birth to death. It is extremely rare. Patton had the 11-2/8 IR set active throughout his entire Life Matrix as seen in his 1st Epoch (11 birth day) and 2nd Epoch (birth month of November), as well as in his 2nd, 3rd and 4th Challenges. Quite noteworthy, this 11-2/8 IR set was the only numeric pattern in his Challenge structure.

A DESTINY BUILT FOR WAR

George Patton's destiny was clearly to be a commanding general. The most telling aspect of his life is depicted in his 44-8 LP and the 11-2/8 IR set in his Life Matrix, which begins at his birth in his 1st Epoch—the day of his birth (the 11th of November) and continues throughout his life, culminating with his 4th Challenge. This 11-2/8 *life linkage*, as noted earlier, shows the energy of war, relationships, adversaries, contention, others and teamwork through the 11-2 energy. This tells us that from his first breath to his last (which for him was age 60), Patton would be heavily challenged with the concept of *others* in its many facets—war being one of them—and the concept of the army as a team. As he has been quoted in his famous "Speech to the Third Army" delivered on the eve of the Allied invasion of France in World War II on the 5th of June 1944 . . . (pattonhq.com/speech)

> *An Army is a team. It lives, sleeps, eats and fights as a team . . .*
>
> *Every man does his job. Every man serves the whole. Every department, every unit, is important in the vast scheme of this war . . .*
>
> *Each man must not think only of himself, but also of his buddy fighting beside him.*

Richard Andrew King

When this 11-2 energy moves through the filter of his 6 Expression, the outcome is an 8 (2 + 6 = 8), the energy of executive management, leadership and command. This combination can be referenced as "war management," which is exactly what Patton did extremely well—manage the battlefield. As Supreme Commander of the Allied forces in Europe, General Dwight D. Eisenhower (later becoming the 34th President of the United States: 1953 to 1961), asserted . . .

> *George Patton was the most brilliant commander of an army*
> *in the open field that our or any other service produced.*

This is certainly high praise, especially coming from a former United States President and five star general who was Patton's commander-in-chief during World War II. Eisenhower's remarks underscore the brilliance of command of Old Blood and Guts.

FLAMBOYANCE & ECCENTRICITY

Patton had a reputation for being both eccentric and flamboyant. The number 5 is largely responsible for the flamboyant aspect. Patton has a 5 PE and a 5 Soul, the former representing the performance he gave in life and the latter identifying his most primal desires. Patton was motivated and driven to be flamboyant, mercurial, diverse, active, freedom-oriented, hard to control and motion/movement-oriented. This 5 energy was further supported by the core of his lifepath—his 55-1 Grand Pinnacle.

The 55-1 is the most unique, original, independent energy of all the master numbers. It is all fire. Interestingly, it is the core of his 44-8 generalship Lifepath, which is all earth. Fire and earth—an interesting combination. Certainly for Patton's adversaries, he created fire in their earth.

When the 1 crown of the 55 funnels through Patton's 6 Expression, the outcome is a 7—the most introspective, thoughtful and studious of the nine basic numbers. This 1/7 IR set is the most solo, solitary, deep-thinking and isolated combination there is. It was this 1/7 combination that gave Patton his enormous ability to study war, which paid great dividends in the victory category. Great fighters must be great thinkers. Patton was a thinker, rash at times and impulsive, but a thinker nonetheless.

Furthermore, the 55-1/7 enregy can make people eccentric because of its powerful originality, independence and depth. Without a doubt, the 55-1 energy does make people unique, as we have discussed many times in this work. When the 7 is in the outcome position, the eccentricity aspect enters into the equation. Without question, George Patton was, indeed, both original and eccentric.

"SMITH" TIMELINE PE: 77-5

Relating to Patton's destiny, from age 40 to 63 he was in the "Smith" Name Timeline which carries a 6/77-5 IR set. The 77-5 master energy reflects a very diverse and active mental process—the 5 being diverse and quick; the 77 being extremely mental, studious, analytical. This energy occurred in the heart of his career, corroborating his skills of conflict, war, tactics, strategies and generalship during World War II.

This 77-5 also contributed to Patton's flamboyance and eccentricity. The 7 energy is the most internal of numbers. When it is elevated eleven times to the 77, the internalization is also expanded, thus helping Patton to be not just flamboyant but the great battlefield tactician he was. Successful warriors must have quick minds, and the 77-5 PE originating from the name "Smith" certainly was a positive asset in this regard.

Name Timeline (NTL): George Smith Patton, Jr.				
	First	Middle #1	Last	Suffix
Names	George	Smith	Patton	Jr.
Timeline	birth to 39	40 to 63	64 to 86	87 to 96
General	39	24	23	10
IR Set	3	6	5	1
	2	5	4	9
Master #s	11	77	22	

ARROGANCE & DOMINANCE

Patton has also been described as arrogant and dominant. The two most powerful numbers acting in concert that create this condition are the 1 and 9. The ego of the 1 and the rulership of the 9 make for a person who is strong, unbending, self-willed, charismatic, dominant, potentially domineering and overbearing, with both leadership and rulership qualities. This 1 and 9 combination is a powerhouse. It often gets people in trouble because the ego can get out of hand, but if a strong leader is the chief ingredient in the recipe for success in difficult times, then the 1 and 9 combination is a workable ticket.

George Patton's Nature was a 1; his Material Nature, a 9. This 1-9 cipher set perfectly expressed Patton's personality—egocentric, strong, dominant, self-willed and overbearing, but also confident, self-assured, action-driven, charismatic and definitely . . . the boss. The 1-9 pairing is who Patton was and he was helpless to change it, just as we are helpless to change the energies (defined by our personal numbers) which drive us and create our destinies.

POWER LEADER

George Patton was a powerful leader. One of the numeric patterns reflecting such leadership is the 22-4/1 IR set which was active in his 1st Pinnacle and 3rd Epoch.

The 22-4 master builder energy is often associated with power and wealth. It also reflects order, discipline, rules, security, solidity, organization, regimentation, conduct, fidelity. It can also be rigid, stubborn and unbending. When filtered through the 6 of Patton's Expression, the outcome of the 22's crown, the 4, is the 1—the number of the ego, self, lone wolf, leader, maverick and pioneer. This 22-4/1 IR set certainly reflected not only Patton's leadership, but his innovative and creative abilities. He was a disciplined individual and he demanded the same from his troops, especially given the fact that he deeply believed the army was a team (2), that every man (1) must do his job (4) and every man (1) must serve the whole (4).

FIERY WORDS, INSPIRATIONAL SPEECHES & COLORFUL LANGUAGE

Patton was no stranger to language that both inspired and inflamed, often drawing praise, criticism and censure. What numbers in his chart reflect this aspect of his life and destiny?

The basic number of communication is the 3. Patton's 2nd Pinnacle and 4th (Crown) Pinnacle are a 33-6/3. This is a positive energy of supportive and personal communication. The problem is that in Patton's chart the 3 is void. Therefore, the 33-6/3 could be written as 3v3v-6/3v to reflect the problematic issues with communication. Still, the energy is there in his chart, so it served Patton well when energizing and inspiring his troops, but contrarily was active in creating harsh, critical, blue-flamed speech which caused him problems throughout his career.

The most famous incident involving the negative expression of Patton's 3 void was the slapping and berating incident of Charles Herman Kuhl, born on 6 November 1915 [Wikipedia], a soldier whom Patton felt was playing ill in order to avoid fighting when other soldiers were bravely placing their lives on the line in combat. Although Kuhl was subsequently diagnosed with malaria after the fact, Patton became irate in the moment, called the soldier a coward, slapped and kicked him. This created an uproar. Patton was forced to apologize to the soldier publicly and was temporarily relieved of his command.

Since this slapping incident was such a scurrilous scar on Patton's career, and since there are no coincidences in the universe, there had to be some numeric connection to it all involving the number 3, and indeed there was. The following bullet-point list highlights the "3 Connections" between Patton, Kuhl and the day of the incident.

Patton & Kuhl – Relationship with the number 3

- The name *Charles* is a 3
- Patton had a 3 void in his chart
- *Old Blood and Guts* is a 57-3 energy
- Patton was 57 years old at the time [57 is a 3 in reduction]
- Patton was a 3 star Lieutenant General at the time of the incident
- The PE of Charles Herman Kuhl's Basic Matrix is a 3
- The Lifepath of Charles Kuhl [6 November 1915] is a 33-6
- The Incident occurred on a 3 calendar day [3 August 1943]
- The incident happened in Patton's 4th Pinnacle: 3v3v-6/3v
- Newspaper columnist Drew Pearson related the story publicly on his radio program on 21 November 1943, another 3 calendar day.
- The name *Drew Pearson* is a 57-3—same as *Old Blood and Guts*

Richard Andrew King

Skeptics may argue the amalgam of 3 instances in the Patton striking incident of Charles Kuhl is merely coincidental. This work takes the viewpoint that nothing is coincidental in this universe and that everything is constructed perfectly by powers beyond our understanding and that such construction is based in numbers and the energies they represent.

The facts in the Patton case are the facts. This concept of *stacking* has been shown already in the lives of both Amelia Earhart's disappearance and Elvis Presley's death. The purpose of relating these *stacking* examples is to show, once again, the relationship between life's events and numbers, which are nothing more than labels for energy fields. Life is not random, and the whole purpose of this book is to present the evidence and let you, the reader, decide for yourself, keeping in mind observations made by two of the greatest scientists in history.

As Pythagoras said,

> *Numbers rule the universe; everything is arranged according to number and mathematical shape.*

And as Newton stated,

> *God created everything by number, weight and measure. It is the perfection of God's works that they are all done with the greatest simplicity. He is the God of order and not of confusion.*

And so it is with life and its events, whether they are slapping incidents, disappearances, deaths or whatever they may be. Numbers tell the tale.

REINCARNATION

George Patton was a staunch believer in reincarnation, having been a soldier in many lives and times. His incarnation as General George S. Patton would seem to bear out the fact that he was destined to live a very specific life. After all, he survived the horror and hell of World War II but then died from complications of a severe cervical spinal cord injury sustained in a fluke auto accident on 21 December 1945. Notice the 3 influence in the day (the 21st) and the month (12th)?

This was only a few months after World War II ended with the formal surrender of the Japanese aboard the deck of the American battleship USS Missouri—2 September 1945 (a 30-3 universal day).

Patton's destiny is very much akin to the destiny of Abraham Lincoln who was elected President of the United States on 6 November 1860, just six weeks before South Carolina succeeded from the Union on 20 December 1860. President Lincoln was fatally shot on the 14th of April 1865 (dying on the 15th), just five days after the Civil War concluded on 9 April 1865 with the surrender of the Confederate Army by General Robert E. Lee to General Ulysses S. Grant at Appomattox, Virginia.

Two great lives; two incredible destinies; two specific assignments. Lincoln's was to create a United States through civil war, and Patton's was to help win a war against a foreign enemy. The point is that as soon as their destined assignments were completed, their lives ended, abruptly— Patton's by a freak accident and Lincoln's by assassination. Coincidence or divine plan? Certainly, Patton believed in personal destiny. Such belief is powerfully proclaimed in his own words . . .

A man must know his destiny... if he does not recognize it, then he is lost.

How many of us know our destiny? How many of us are lost? If we were to study our numbers, and thereby recognize our destiny, we would not be, as Patton states, lost. Furthermore, we would fulfill the ancient Greek aphorism, *Know Thyself*, and, in keeping with the teachings of high level mystics, we must become self-realized before we can become God-realized. Thus, knowing our own personal set of numbers will be a valuable asset in managing our life and its future because we will eventually reap the fruit of the seeds we sow now. Knowing ourselves and our destiny cannot but give us a great advantage in the game of life.

Regarding his belief in his own reincarnation, Patton penned a poem entitled, "Through a Glass Darkly." For brevity's sake, the first and final stanzas are offered here, stanzas which clearly reflect Patton's belief in reincarnation.

Richard Andrew King

Through a Glass, Darkly
George S. Patton, Jr.
(full poem is 24 stanzas)

(1st Stanza)

Through the travail of the ages,

Midst the pomp and toil of war,

Have I fought and strove and perished

Countless times upon this star.

(last Stanza)

So forever in the future,

Shall I battle as of yore,

Dying to be born a fighter,

But to die again, once more.

Do Patton's numbers reveal a belief in reincarnation? Not necessarily, but what they do reveal is a highly unique individual who is his own person, as witnessed by his 1 Nature supported by his 55-1 Grand Pinnacle with its 7 PE. No two numbers in tandem reflect independent thought and isolation more than the 1 and 7. His 77 PE in his Name Timeline of "Smith" indicates much introspective and reflective thought, corroborating his Grand Pinnacle 7 PE. Too, his 2/8 Challenge grouping indicates a deep intuitive connection and this 2/8 IR set is the only Challenge energy in Patton's chart. None of these number patterns necessarily indicate a belief in reincarnation, but they do support a deep, intuitive, internal and reflective connection beyond the norm.

DEATH: 8/(8)/7 LTL – "H" of "SMITH"

George Patton died at the age of 60 in the "H" Letter Timeline of his second name, "Smith." This "H" carried an 8/7 IR set, one of the most challenging combinations in numerology. It's extended ciphering is 8/(8)/16-7. Of significance is that it is the only 8/(8)/7 IR set in his Letter Timeline. Unlike Amelia Earhart and Elvis Presley, whose deaths were dramatic, there was nothing of major numerical note at the time of Patton's death except for the timing and nature of it—coming shortly after World War II ended and as a result of a freak vehicle accident. On a second note, it is interesting to see the complications, trials, travails, tribulations, tragedies, testings and problems reflected when the 7 is in the Reality position of an IR set. Something to ponder.

SUMMARY

George Smith Patton Jr. was an intriguing individual and a great general—enigmatic and eccentric, charismatic and caustic, flamboyant and fiery. He was unique, demanding, egocentric, courageous, brave—a true living legend in his own time who created an aura that can only be called the *Patton Mystique*.

Some of the interesting components in the numerology chart of General George S. Patton, Jr. are . .
.

- All of the components of General Patton's Life Matrix—the framework of his 44-8 Lifepath—house master numbers except his 1st Challenge, which has no cipher whatsoever. This is a result of his 11 November birthday (11 minus 11 = 0)

- Patton's Grand (3rd) Pinnacle is a 55-1 (core of his 44-8 LP)

- Patton's 2nd Pinnacle and Crown (4th) Pinnacle are a 33-6

- All of Patton's Epochs are master numbers

- All of Patton's Name Timeline PEs house a master number

- Patton's Life Matrix consists of a quintstack of 11-2/8 energy creating life linkage—three sets in his 2nd, 3rd and 4th Challenges and two in his 1st and 2nd Epochs (Note: the 8 PE of this IR set matches his 8 Lifepath with its 44 master root)

- Every one of Patton's Life Challenges reveals conflict, teamwork and relationship (11-2), generalship and command (8)

- The word "General" is an 8 matching his simple Lifepath

- Patton died in the only 8/(8)/7 Letter Timeline in his life, the "H" of "Smith"

- Interestingly, the word *military* is a 44-8 energy, matching Patton's Lifepath.

Richard Andrew King

(Photo courtesy of Wikipedia)

GENERAL GEORGE S. PATTON, JR – QUOTES

A man must know his destiny… if he does not recognize it, then he is lost.

I am a soldier, I fight where I am told and I win where I fight.

If everybody is thinking alike, then somebody isn't thinking.

In war the only sure defense is offense.

Keep punching.

There is a time to take counsel of your fears and there is a time to never listen to any fear.

You're never beaten until you admit it.

Fixed fortifications are monuments to man's stupidity.

Live for something rather than die for nothing.

There is only one type of discipline, perfect discipline.

No sane man is unafraid in battle, but discipline produces in him a form of vicarious courage.

War is the supreme test of man in which he rises to heights never approached in any other activity.

An Army is a team. It lives, sleeps, eats and fights as a team.

Lead me, follow me, or get out of my way.

Never let the enemy pick the battle site.

It's the unconquerable soul of man, not the nature of the weapon he uses, that insures victory.

In case of doubt, attack.

I always believe in being prepared, even when I'm dressed in white tie and tails.

Always do more than is required of you.

War is simple, direct and ruthless.

Richard Andrew King

HISTORIC ICON #5

HOWARD HUGHES

Born: Howard Robard Hughes, Jr. – 24 December 1905

Died – 5 April 1976, age 70

[Note: Actual birth date is in question. Hughes states he was born on 24 December. Baptismal records indicate 24 September. This treatise has chosen 24 December because its numbers more accurately depict the life of Howard Hughes.]

----

* Congressional Gold Medal, 1939

In recognition of the achievements of Howard Hughes in advancing the science of aviation and thus bringing great credit to his country throughout the world.

(Photo courtesy of Wikimedia Commons)

Richard Andrew King

H oward Hughes was a true American original and arguably the most famous eccentric recluse in modern world history. Billionaire, pioneer, record-setting aviator, movie producer and director, engineer, industrialist, philanthropist and legendary womanizer—all are ingredients of the Howard Hughes mystique. What kind of numerology chart must such an individual have to manifest such a diverse, successful, extraordinary but eccentric life? Here are a few germane questions.

PROVOCATIVE QUESTIONS

- What master number identifies Hughes' extreme wealth?
- What master number illustrates his originality?
- Which numbers reveal his eccentricity and public seclusion?
- Which number pattern expresses his movie accomplishments?
- Which numerical patterns create double lifetime linkage?
- What numbers reveal his romantic proclivities?

HOWARD HUGHES AND THE NUMBERS OF WEALTH

One number stands above all the rest in expressing massive wealth—the *Master Builder* number 22, the addcap of which is a 4. The number 2 is the root number of money because it represents barter, an exchange of one item for another. Money is simply the medium of barter. The number 2 also rules relationship, partnership and exchange. Money is the current means of commercial exchange of goods and services in relationship. When 2 is multiplied eleven times, the result is 22—a powerful elevation of the 2's inherent qualities. Too, the addcap or crown of the 22 is the 4 which represents security, especially economic security in the form of power and wealth. The 4 also represents work, service and mechanical aptitude.

Howard Hughes had a quintset (five set) of the 22-4 master builder energy in his chart which included a very rare double 22-4 in his PE or Performance/Experience—the reality of his life, the role he would be giving on the great life stage. In other words, a role of power and wealth. Combined with this double 22-4, which can be written as 22^2-4, his most primal desire, his Soul, is a 22-4 as well. We can see this clearly in his Basic Matrix.

Basic Matrix: Howard Robard Hughes, Jr.

LP	Exp.	PE	Soul	MS	Nature	MN	Voids
6	7	22^2 - 4	22-4	55-1	3	99-9	none

Beyond this triset of 22-4 energy in his Basic Matrix, Howard Hughes' 1st Epoch PE and his 3rd (last/crown) Epoch PE are also 22-4s. All of this translates into a life reality of great wealth. And to be clear, such a large amount of 22-4 energy in a chart is uncommon and defines his historic wealth and power, as well as his work ethic and all things mechanical.

ORIGINALITY

By now, it's fair to ask the question, "Which master number represents originality more than any other master number?" If your answer is the 55-1, you are correct. Every featured individual in this work had the 55-1 Master Explorer/Creator energy present in their King's Numerology[tm] chart (birth chart or common name chart), and all of them were extremely unconventional, unique, original and one-of-a-kind icons—Albert Einstein, Amelia Earhart, Elvis Presley, George Patton, Howard Hughes, John F. Kennedy, Marilyn Monroe, Michael Jackson, Muhammad Ali, Oprah Winfrey, Princess Diana and Sarah Palin.

Howard Hughes had a triset (3 set) of 55-1 in his chart—Material Soul, Crown Pinnacle PE and his Name Timeline PE of "Robard." One 55-1 master energy is notable, but three are extraordinary. Because Hughes had the 55-1 in his Material Soul, he deeply wanted to be unconventional, unique, original, a trend setter, a one-of-a-kind pioneer—all of which he most definitely was, undeniably. The number 5 governs speed and, hence, the 55-1 master energy was a major force in his aeronautics achievements and list of "firsts."

Hughes' Crown Pinnacle 55-1 PE in his Life Matrix guaranteed a life that was both original and unconventional. His 55-1 Name Timeline PE of "Robard" was active between ages 34 and 64—a thirty-one year period in the center of his life. Obviously, this triset proved very powerful in making him extremely unique.

Richard Andrew King

This 55-1 combined with his 22-4 had a marked influence on Hughes' design and engineering aptitude. 1 rules creation. 4 rules structural design. So much of Hughes' personality was to design, create and innovate.

MOVIE MOGUL

The 1 energy likes to be first, to be a leader, achiever, pioneer, star, icon. The 1 is the number of the self, identity and ego. The 55-1 pattern speaks to being the best at what one does. Still, there's more to Hughes' 1 energy than simply the 55-1.

The number governing images and pictures—still or moving—is the 3, the energy of self-expression, joy, fun, play, beauty, health, communication, sex and children. Other than the triset of 55-1 energy, Hughes also has a rare lifetime linkage of 3/1 energy—his 1st and 2nd Challenge, 2nd Epoch and 4th Pinnacle. The 2nd Epoch, 1st and 2nd Challenge IR sets form a triangle which is clearly visible in his Life Matrix (following).

It is this lifetime 3/1 linkage that had a direct bearing on Hughes' success in the movie business. His 99-9 Nature also gave him a universal and theatrical energy set which helped him produce hits such as *Everybody's Acting*, *Two Arabian Knights*, *The Racket*, *The Front Page*, *Hell's Angels*, *Scarface* and *The Outlaw*.

All this 1 energy may be one of the reasons for Hughes' statement:

> *I intend to be the greatest golfer in the world,*
> *the finest film producer in Hollywood,*
> *the greatest pilot in the world,*
> *and the richest man in the world.*

One of the axioms of The King's Numerology^{tm} is that *we all speak our numbers*. Often, we are not conscious of what we're saying unless we have an intimate understanding of our own numbers. It is doubtful that Hughes had a working knowledge of numerology but, yet, his quote above certainly reveals that he was *speaking his numbers*. Having a lifetime linkage of 3/1 energy certainly allowed him to make great achievements in his life.

ECCENTRICITY, PUBLIC SECLUSION AND MENTAL ANGUISH

A major part of Hughes' mystique was his eccentricity, no doubt. He was one of the most mysterious individuals in modern world history. One of the number patterns responsible for this was the 55-1. It always makes people unique, different and unconventional, but reclusive? Solo maybe but not reclusive, at least to the extent Hughes was.

The main number pattern for Hughes' reclusion, eccentricity and mental suffering is the 9/7 IR set which, like the 3/1 IR set, manifested lifetime linkage, occupying his 1st, 2nd and 3rd Pinnacle, as well as his 3rd and 4th Challenges. The concentration of this 9/7 pattern was intensified because it occupied both his Grand Pinnacle and Grand Challenge—the *Grand PC Couplet*, the center or core of his 6 Lifepath. Because this 9/7 began at birth, it continued to grow, just like a tree, taking on more severe traits the older he became, extending and exacerbating his suffering, anguish and isolation.

Too, Hughes' Expression was a 7, the most reclusive of all numbers. The Soul of "Howard" and "Robard" are identical 7s (O & A), thus intensifying his need for privacy and reclusion. These 7s had a direct bearing on him being a shy and retiring individual who shunned publicity, especially in his later years.

The number 7 also represents traits of perfectionism. It has been said that Hughes' attention to detail was immaculate. This goes directly to the continuing amount of 7 energy in his chart. People with an abundance of 4 and 7 energy in their charts make good engineers, scientists, mathematicians, accountants, analysts, researchers, editors—anyone associated with *structural analysis*.

This 9/7 lifetime linkage containing both the Grand Pinnacle and Grand Challenge is extremely unusual. One applicable phrase for the 9/7 IR set is *public reclusion* or *reclusion from the public* (the 9 representing the *public* and the 7 representing *reclusion*). The number 7 is the most inward-

Richard Andrew King

dwelling energy and therefore the most private, secretive, recessive. In the 9/7 IR set, in order to arrive at the 7, the 9 (the influencing energy) must pass through Hughes' 7 Expression to create the 7 outcome energy. One way to denote this is 9/(7)/7 (9 + 7 = 16: 1 + 6 = 7). In other words, there is an abundance of private and seclusive energy in the 9/7 IR sets of his life and names. One of the very rare things regarding Hughes' chart is the double set of life linkage as reflected in the 3/1 and 9/7 IR sets.

LIFE MATRIX
Voids: none
HOWARD ROBARD HUGHES, JR.
24 DECEMBER 1905

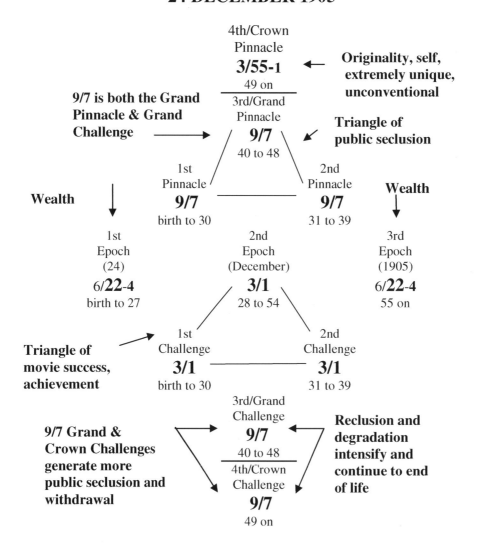

Note 1: this is an amazing chart showing double Lifetime Linkage of the 3/1 and 9/7—both revealing triangular structures within the Life Matrix. Note 2: 9/7 occupies Hughes' Grand PC Couplet (3rd Pinnacle *and* 3rd Challenge), the center of his Lifepath.

LOVE AND ROMANCE

Howard Hughes had the reputation of being a notorious ladies' man and womanizer. Allegedly, he had affairs with such famous women as Katharine Hepburn, Ava Gardner, Bette Davis, Ginger Rogers, Olivia de Havilland, Gene Tierney and others. He was officially married twice and allegedly a third time. His first wife was Ella Rice from 1925 to 1929. The "alleged" wife was Terry Moore from 1949 to 1976 (a claim she made after his death) and Jean Peters from 1957 to 1971 (Wikipedia).

Which numbers in Hughes' chart reveal such an amorous nature? The master numbers 33 and 66 certainly played a major role, especially the 33—the most pleasure-saturated of all master numbers.

Hughes' chart shows a *quintset* (set of five) of 33 energy—the name of "Howard" itself (active from birth through age 33) and a *quadset* (set of four) of 33 PEs related to the four "Rs" in his full birth name.

The 66 master number manifested as a triset (set of three) in the PE of his first name of "Howard" and in the PEs associated with the "O" in both "Howard" and "Robard."

The energy of romance is clearly visible in the Name Timeline of "Howard," which carries a powerful master IR set of 33/66 [simple: 6/3]

Richard Andrew King

	First	Middle #1	Last	Suffix
Name Timeline (NTL): Howard Robard Hughes, Jr.				
Names	Howard	Robard	Hughes	Jr.
Timeline	birth to 33	34 to 64	65 to 96	97 to 106
General	*33	31	32	10
IR Set	6	4	5	1
	3	1	2	7
Master #s	*33 & 66	55	11	

Howard Hughes piloting the Spruce Goose

(Photo courtesy of Wikimedia Commons)

MASTER NUMBERS – HOWARD ROBARD HUGHES, JR.

Following is a list of the master numbers in Hughes' chart.

Master Numbers in Howard Hughes' Chart	
11	"Hughes" Name Timeline PE
22	*Quintset* (appears 5 times)
	PE - Double 22s (highly unusual)
	Soul – 22
	1st Epoch PE
	3rd Epoch PE
33	*Quintset* (appears 5 times)
	"Howard" (birth to 33)
	Quadset "R" Letter Timeline PEs in his full name
44	none
55	*Triset* (appears 3 times)
	Material Soul
	"Robard" PE (ages 34 to 64)
	Crown Pinnacle PE
66	*Triset*
	"Howard" PE (birth to 33)
	"O" Letter Timeline PE of "Howard" (ages 9 to 14)
	"O" Letter Timeline PE of "Robard" (ages 43 to 48)
77	none
88	none
99	Material Nature

Richard Andrew King

SUMMARY

Howard Hughes was as brilliant as he was troubled. His accomplishments and behaviors speak for themselves and his numbers. He was also a generous man. There are many accounts of him helping various people throughout his life. Such generosity is associated with the 9 energy. The Material Nature of Hughes was an expansive 99-9, magnifying a benevolent disposition. Where have we seen this before?

Hughes' contributions to society included *Hughes Aircraft, Hughes Space and Communications Co., Hughes Electronics Corp.* and the *Howard Hughes Medical Institute* devoted to biological and medical research.

Combined with his aviation exploits and movie accomplishments, Hughes' legacy will remain rich while he remains forever as the most mysteriously famous person of the late 20th Century.

Some interesting components in Hughes' chart are . . .

- Double *lifetime linkage* of the 3/1 and 9/7 IR sets
- The 3/1 and 9/7 IR sets form visual triangles in his Life Matrix
- 9/7 is both his Grand Pinnacle & Grand Challenge—life's core
- *Quintset* of 9/7 in his Life Matrix
- *Quintset* of 22-4 master builder energy
- *Quadset* of 3/1 energy in his Life Matrix
- Double 22s in his life Performance/Experience [PE]
- *Quintset* of 33-6 master imaginator/communicator energy
- *Triset* of 55-1 master explorer/creator energy
- *Triset* of 66-3 master lover/artisan energy
- Identical 7s in the Soul of *Howard* and *Robard*

HOWARD HUGHES – QUOTES

I want to be remembered for only one thing – my contribution to aviation.

I intend to be the greatest golfer in the world, the finest film producer in Hollywood, the greatest pilot in the world and the richest man in the world.

I am by nature a perfectionist, and I seem to have trouble allowing anything to go through in a half-perfect condition.

I'm not a paranoid deranged millionaire. Goddamit, I'm a billionaire.

My father told me, never have partners.

Every man has his price or a guy like me couldn't exist.

Play off everyone against each other so that you have more avenues of action open to you.

Once you consent to some concession, you can never cancel it and put things back the way they are.

The door to the cabinet is to be opened using a minimum of 15 Kleenexes.

Richard Andrew King

HISTORIC ICON #6

J O H N F. K E N N E D Y (JFK)

Born: John Fitzgerald Kennedy – 29 May 1917

Died – 22 November 1963 by Assassination, age 46

----

* 35th President of the United States of America—1961 to 1963

* Youngest elected President, age 43

* Navy and Marine Corps Medal recipient, 1943, awarded for

Distinguishing oneself by heroism not involving actual conflict with an enemy.

For acts of lifesaving, or attempted lifesaving, it is required

that the action be performed at the risk of one's own life.

(Official Presidential Portrait)

Richard Andrew King

He was young, rich, dynamic and charismatic—a modern day iconic King of Camelot whose tragic death would befit a Shakespearean drama and leave a legacy of hidden adulterous affairs and a conspiracy of assassination that, unlike him, would never die. He was the youngest man ever elected to the Presidency of the United States of America at the age of forty-three. America's 35th Commander-in-Chief, he was John Fitzgerald Kennedy, notably known by his initials, JFK.

Kennedy's Presidency was saturated with tumult, marked by such events as the construction of the Berlin Wall by the USSR (Union of Soviet Socialist Republics) in 1961, the bungled Bay of Pigs Invasion (also in 1961), the Cuban Missile Crisis (1962), the Space Race between America and the Soviet Union (which began in 1957 with the launching of Sputnik by the USSR), the on-going American Civil Rights Movement and the incipient stages of the Vietnam War. Perhaps the most horrendous event was his conspiracy-laden assassination on 22 November 1963 in Dealey Plaza, Dallas, Texas, at the age of 46—an event that shocked America and changed a nation forever.

John Fitzgerald Kennedy, also known personally as "Jack," was born on 29 May 1917. He served as President of the United States from his inauguration on 20 January 1961 (age 43) to his assassination on 22 November 1963 (age 46), a total of exactly 1037 days. Hence, his time in office is often referred to as the 1,000 Day Presidency. For such a relatively short time it was one of the most intense and problem-strewn White House occupancies ever, not simply on a national and international level but also on a personal basis. With such a presidential experience, what are some of the provocative questions that can be asked relative to his King's Numerology™ chart?

PROVOCATIVE QUESTIONS

- What master number drove Kennedy's ambition?
- What does Kennedy's 7 Lifepath reveal about his life's journey?
- Does Kennedy's chart reveal a 55-1 master energy?
- What is common to George Washington and JFK's presidencies?
- What number pattern reveals his secret love affairs?
- What is unusual about JFK's Grand & Crown Challenge cipher set?
- What is significant regarding the date of JFK's assassination?

JFK – BASIC MATRIX

The first clues to Kennedy's life are seen in his Basic Matrix.

Basic Matrix: John Fitzgerald Kennedy

LP	Exp.	PE	Soul	MS	Nature	MN	Voids
7	8	33-6	11-2	99-9	6	22-4	none

Kennedy's ambition and attraction to public life is clearly visible in his 99-9 Material Soul, defining a desire to be a man of power, to move upon the universal life stage and be in the public eye. The ambition of power and rulership is at its zenith in the 99-9 master energy. Therefore, Kennedy loved being in a power position and truth be told—he most probably loved being President of the United States of America, the most powerful office in the world, and thus arguably making him the most powerful man in the world.

Softening the potentially harsh aspects of the 99-9 is the personal love energy of Kennedy's 6 Nature and 33-6 PE which, although sexually charged (more on this later), reference the family—whether that family is a small unit of a few individuals, a community or a nation. Certainly, Kennedy was very popular with a vast number of Americans and this 6 energy was a major factor in people's love and admiration for him.

JFK's Lifepath is a 7—the most inherently tragic, turbulent, sorrowful, tearful, heartbreaking, heart wrenching and secretive of the nine basic life scripts. It is a very difficult Lifepath. Ironically, it is also the one containing the most spiritual energy and opportunity for substantive growth. Diamonds are made under extreme heat and pressure over an extended period of time, not by a mere and casual blowing of an intermittent wind. If a soul is to rise to the crystalline brilliance and strength of a diamond, it must be subjected to heat, pressure and time. It is the reality of life. As Winston Churchill beautifully stated, *Kites rise highest against the wind, not with it.*

Therefore, from the get-go it was obvious Kennedy's destiny would place him in difficult and challenging positions, both publically and personally, positions which would test his spirituality,

Richard Andrew King

nobility, character, ethics and morality. It was this 7 Lifepath that housed the tumultuous framework of his professional life, personal tragedies and presidential challenges.

Kennedy's Expression is an 8, the number of administration, organization, orchestration, coordination and connection—the exact energy necessary for an executive. This served him well as a public servant, especially given his 99-9 Material Soul and 22-4 Material Nature of service to the public.

The 11-2 Soul identifies a desire for relationship, partnership, competition, opposition, adversarial involvement and Yin (female) energy. This, unquestionably, was a factor in Kennedy's involvement with others. He embraced relationship, whether it was pleasant or adversarial. The master 22-4 Material Nature reveals a personality focused on structure, order, wealth and security. It is conventional, traditional, work and service-oriented—an excellent energy to have as a leader.

KENNEDY'S UNIQUENESS

Jack Kennedy was unique. No doubt about it. He was a true original, trend setter and leader. Which master number reflects these qualities? If you answered the 55-1, you're right. JFK's 55-1 master energy occupied his Crown Pinnacle PE (see Life Matrix), the same location as that of Howard Hughes. The difference is that Kennedy's 55-1 PE stems from the 2 energy of others and relationship while Hughes' PE originated from the 3 energy of communication, image and media. Therefore, JFK's leadership and uniqueness is a derivative of *relationship* (in all its aspects— harmonious and contentious) and *others* (friend or foe) while Hughes' 55-1 emanated from the 3 energy of self-expression, art, media, image, well-being, pleasure and communication.

THE KENNEDY-WASHINGTON CONNECTION

There are some notable connections between John F. Kennedy, the 35th President of the United States, and George Washington, the 1st President in America's history. This would be expected of individuals who share powerful presidential legacies.

The 88 Master Number

The name "George Washington" is an 88-7. Kennedy's Name Timeline of "Fitzgerald" carries an 88 PE (NTL chart). As we know, 8 reflects administration, connection and organization—in effect, the *flow* of energy. As a master number, the 88-7 houses both powerfully positive and negative aspects. It can be very noble and spiritual or ignoble and worldly. The thing of note is that it is an extremely connective and interactive energy, whether its connections are divine or demonic. No number is more connective than the 8. It knows how to orchestrate, coordinate and get things done. This is why people with 8s in their charts often make very good managers, administrators, executives, personal assistants, mechanics—anyone who can understand the interrelationship and flow of a process from inception to completion. Other famous or infamous individuals with the number 88 in their charts are: Albert Einstein, Albert Schweitzer, Nikola Tesla, Mother Teresa, Elvis Presley, Henry Wadsworth Longfellow, John Wooden, Michael Phelps, the United States of America, Warren Buffett, Joseph Stalin, Jared Lee Loughner and John Edwards.

Name Timeline (NTL): John Fitzgerald Kennedy			
	First	Middle	Last
Names	John	Fitzgerald	Kennedy
Timeline	birth to 20	21 to 74	75 to 107
General	20	54	33
IR Set	2	9 (54-Exp)	6
	9	7 (34-LP)	4
Master #s		88-16-7	22

JFK's 2nd Name Timeline of "Fitzgerald" was the period of his presidency and assassination. The 9/7 IR set with its underlying 88 master root threatened trouble and tragedy which, unfortunately, came to pass.

The 1/9 and 9/1 Juxtaposition

Another interesting connection between George Washington and John Kennedy are the 1/9 and 9/1 IR sets which reference leadership (1) of the public (9). Both of Washington's and JFK's charts reveal this 1-9 numerical combination during the exact time of their presidencies.

Richard Andrew King

Washington served as president from age 57 to 65 (30 April 1789 to 4 March 1797). This was primarily during his 9/1 Letter Timeline (LTL) of the "I" in "Washington" from age 55 to 63. Kennedy served as president from age 43 to 46 (20 January 1961 to 22 November 1963) during his Grand Challenge timeline which housed a 1/9 IR set—the only timeline in his chart which revealed this 1/9 pattern.

The difference between the 1/9 and 9/1 is the numeric filter which colors the outcome. For example, Kennedy's Grand Challenge 1/9 IR set is derived from the 1 of the self, action and leadership passing through his 8 Expression to create the 9 (1 + 8 = 9). His 1/9 IR set could therefore be written as 1/(8)/9.

Washington's Letter Timeline 9/1 IR set is derived from the initiating and influencing power of the 9 passing through his 1 Lifepath (9 + 1 = 10: 1 + 0 = 1). Therefore, his 9/1 could be ciphered as 9/(1)/1. Thus, the difference between the 1/9 and 9/1 is the number which acts as the filter or funnel through which the initiating *influence* number must pass to create the outcome *reality* number of the IR set. Still, both the 1/9 and 9/1 address leadership, the self and the public. [For more on IR sets and filters, consult *The King's Book of Numerology II: Forecasting – Part 1*].

SECRET LOVE AFFAIRS

It is common knowledge that JFK engaged in continuous adulterous activity during his marriage to his wife, Jacqueline Kennedy. There is his pre-marital relationship and post-wedding affair with Gunilla von Post. Perhaps most famous is his relationship with Marilyn Monroe. Other women often connected to JFK are Judith Campbell, Mary Pinchot Meyer and Mimi Beardsley Alford. (Wikipedia)

Kennedy's chart clearly reveals the potential for such behavior in multiple places. First, the numbers forming his Basic Matrix Umbrella—his 7 Lifepath, 8 Expression and 6 Performance/Experience (PE) with its 33 master root reveal a red flag. Too, his quintset (set of five) of 33 energy throughout his chart is another. His 7/33-6 IR Sets occupying his Basic Matrix Umbrella, 1st Pinnacle, Grand Challenge and Crown Challenge are others. All of these numerical patterns create warning signals of untoward behavior, betrayal and potential adultery. While they may not guarantee it across the spectrum of relationships, they certainly indicate the potential of such behaviors.

The 7-8-6 Umbrella

The 7-8-6 energy pattern comprises Kennedy's Basic Matrix Umbrella. When the 7 Lifepath lessons of spiritual, ethical and moral testing, with its cloak of privacy and secrecy, filter through the 8 Expression of connection, interaction and involvement, the outcome reality is the 6 of personal love (or lust) and romance. When the 6 also has a 33 master root (signifying intense pleasure-seeking) attached to it (which it doesn't always have), the scenario is a recipe ripe for untoward and adulterous behavior.

JFK was not the first person beset with this 7-8-6 umbrella pattern, nor will he be the last. It is a dangerous combination *if* the person living it does not imbue the highest ideals of spirituality, ethical conduct and purity of behavior. One simple phrase for this set could be "secret love connections." Another phrase is "adulterous love." Yet another could be "romantic heartache," and still another, "family tragedy." All of these phrases fit this Basic Matrix Umbrella 7-8-6 pattern. While many factors in a chart have an influence on how the energies of this triumvirate are manifested, the potential for broken vows, broken homes, broken hearts and broken bonds of love are quite possible. Kennedy's life is a perfect example of how this specific pattern can affect a person's life. As a note, betrayals and untoward behavior are not limited to this 7-8-6 triset. It is just one of those patterns that carries an automatic red flag.

The 7/33-6 Grand & Crown Challenges

Kennedy's 3rd and 4th Challenges (Grand and Crown respectively) contain this same IR set associated with his umbrella, thus exacerbating and magnifying its power, creating a *stacking* of its energies. As we have learned, stacking creates intensity. Since this 7/33-6 pattern already exists in his Basic Matrix (in simple form as the 7-8-6 triset), having it also located in the Grand and Challenge positions of his chart is not a good sign. The Grand Challenge is the centermost core of his 7 Lifepath along with his 3/2 Grand Pinnacle, which is not as troublesome. Challenges in a chart usually reveal the most difficulty and they are generally hidden from view. As history bears witness, the extent of Kennedy's personal and family issues were not fully known until after his death.

The 33 Quintset

Creating more fuel to Kennedy's personal life was the quintset of 33 energy pervading his chart. It is located in the name "Kennedy," his Life Performance/Experience (PE), First Pinnacle PE, Grand Challenge PE and Crown Challenge PE. When a number, especially a master number, appears five times in a chart its effects—positive or negative—will be noticeable.

The 33 binary is known as the *Master Imaginator/Communicator* in The King's Numerology[tm]. Yes, it does have its sexual and sensual aspect but it also represents great ability to communicate with words, art, voice, dance and so forth. Kennedy was an excellent speaker and many of his quotations have become solidified in the American political landscape. Perhaps his most iconic quotation is:

> *My fellow Americans, ask not what your country can do for you; ask what you can do for your country.*

As we're seeing, the charts of our featured icons reveal multiple identical energy patterns, many of which are master numbers such as the 33. It is this amalgam of master power that helped create who and what they were or are. Master numbers are a dominant numerical framework of their destinies, destinies comprised of energies which are always dual in nature, intrinsically housing forces that are simultaneously positive and negative and which . . . for the wise individual . . . demand introspection and reflection.

Official White House portrait of John F. Kennedy

(Aaron Shikler)

MASTER NUMBERS – JOHN FITZGERALD KENNEDY

See following page.

Master Numbers in JFK'S Chart	
11	Soul
	1st House of self, ego, action, leadership
	First Epoch
	Crown Pinnacle
	Grand Pinnacle PE
	Grand Challenge
	Crown Challenge
22	Name Timeline PE of "Kennedy"
	Material Nature
	Second Epoch PE
	Second Pinnacle PE
33	Name "Kennedy"
	Life Performance/Experience (PE)
	First Pinnacle PE
	Grand & Crown Challenge PEs
44	none
55	Crown Pinnacle PE
66	none
77	none
88	Name Timeline PE of "Fitzgerald"
	Grand & Crown Challenges – 1888 [tri-master root]
99	Material Soul

JFK's GRAND CHALLENGE CIPHER SET (ages 39 to 47)

The Grand Challenge is the core Challenge of a person's Lifepath. Normally, a person will have one or two Challenges. JFK's chart has three IR sets, an uncommon aspect but not unknown. In simple ciphers, the three IR sets contained within his Grand Challenge are: 1/9, 2/1 and 7/6. Because of their power and significance, when master numbers exist in a Challenge, they should be referenced. For example, an 11 is a 2 in reduction and all 11s therefore are 2s. However, all 2s are not necessarily 11s. 11 is 11, just as 33 is 33, even though it can be reduced to a crown (simple number) of 6.

Kennedy's three IR sets in his Grand Challenge illustrate the complexity of his life during the period of his Presidency.

3rd/Grand Challenge

Ages 39 to 47

Timeline of his Presidency and Assassination

1/9 & 11-2/1 & 7/33-6

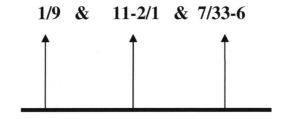

JFK: Grand Challenges

A. 1/9—the self in a leadership position, i.e. President of the U.S.

B. 11-2/1—reveals relationship intensity of the self and leadership

C. 7/33-6—illustrates tribulations and secrecy in the domestic/love life

Richard Andrew King

LIFE MATRIX
Voids: none
JOHN FITZGERALD KENNEDY
29 MAY 1917

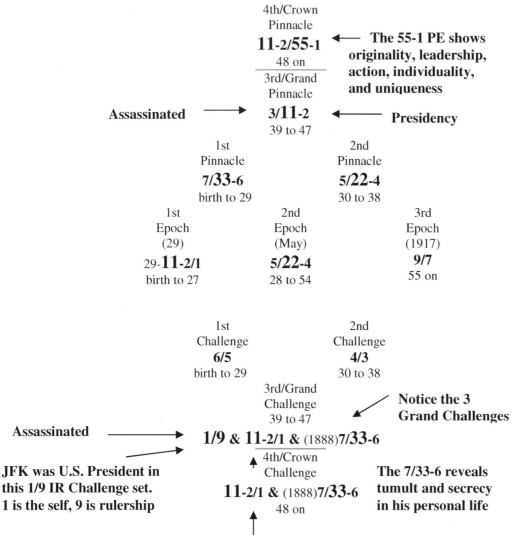

4th/Crown
Pinnacle
11-2/55-1 ← **The 55-1 PE shows originality, leadership, action, individuality, and uniqueness**
48 on

3rd/Grand
Pinnacle
Assassinated → **3/11-2** ← **Presidency**
39 to 47

1st Pinnacle	2nd Pinnacle
7/33-6	**5/22-4**
birth to 29	30 to 38

1st Epoch (29)	2nd Epoch (May)	3rd Epoch (1917)
29-**11-2/1**	**5/22-4**	**9/7**
birth to 27	28 to 54	55 on

1st Challenge	2nd Challenge
6/5	**4/3**
birth to 29	30 to 38

3rd/Grand
Challenge
39 to 47 ← **Notice the 3 Grand Challenges**

Assassinated →
→ **1/9 & 11-2/1 & (1888)7/33-6**

JFK was U.S. President in this 1/9 IR Challenge set. 1 is the self, 9 is rulership

4th/Crown
Challenge
11-2/1 & (1888)7/33-6
48 on

The 7/33-6 reveals tumult and secrecy in his personal life

The 11-2/1 indicates opposition (2) focusing on leadership and the self

THE KENNEDY ASSASSINATION

The assassination of JFK on 22 November 1963 was a remarkable event in American history—in many ways an unbelievable, horrific and unspeakably tragic drama. Arguably, the only other event of such magnitude in the late Twentieth and early Twenty-First Centuries would be the attack on the World Trade Center Towers on 11 September 2001, aka 9/11.

A Personal Note

I was a Sophomore in high school at the time of the JFK assassination. It was a Friday. I was walking from one class to another when I heard the news. It was pure shock. President Kennedy assassinated? How could this be? Everyone was stunned—students and teachers alike.

That entire weekend I was glued to our black and white television. Color TV did not exist then. There were no cordless phones, cell phones, computers or other personal communication devices in those days, those days of yore. Nor was there the type of everyday violence, tension, division and unease that exists today. It was a more innocent time but a time whose innocence was waning as the Cold War between the USA and the USSR was waxing. The Cuban Missile Crisis had just occurred a year earlier—an event that brought the world to the edge of nuclear war closer than it had ever been. But still there was a sense of innocence left. After all, it was a time of Camelot, of the handsome King (Jack) and his Queen (Jacqueline). Too, kids in my generation had never seen war, having been born after World War II.

Watching the news that weekend was a time neither I, nor those of my generation, will ever forget. For those who are still alive, it's a good bet every one of them knew exactly where they were when they received the shock that the President of the United States had been fatally shot. It was poignantly painful, just like 9/11 for this generation.

That weekend was eerie. The only major news channels—ABC, CBS and NBC were awash in images of men and women openly weeping in the streets, stunned in their grief. JFK was a popular, charismatic, articulate, beloved President. And now gone? It was numbingly surreal.

Richard Andrew King

Sunday morning, 24 November, added more drama. I remember watching Lee Harvey Oswald, Kennedy's alleged assassin, being escorted by the police through the Dallas Police Headquarters and ultimately through its basement en route to the county jail when Jack Ruby, a Dallas night club owner, moved through the crowd (from right to left) and fatally shot Oswald at point blank range in the stomach. Shock! Another murder in real time on national television! Today, people only see clips of the shooting. For us who saw the event in real time and who are still alive, watching that murder unfold now is not just a clip of history, it was, for us at the time, history in the making.

Sunday's events did not terminate with Ruby's shooting of Oswald in the morning. In the afternoon, Kennedy's funeral cortège, with his flag-covered casket transported by a horse-drawn caisson poignantly accompanied by a riderless horse (Blackjack) with stirrups reversed to acknowledge a fallen warrior, proceeded from the White House along Pennsylvania Avenue to the Capitol Rotunda as multitudes of people lined the boulevard. Then, as his body lay in state, hundreds of thousands of people lined up outside the Capitol and patiently entered the building, filing past his coffin, paying their final respects. What I remember—which was quite nice but nonetheless eerie—was the silence of it all, that and the event's iconic images of his wife and daughter, Caroline, kneeling beside his coffin as Jacqueline kissed it. Then there was the image of his three year old son, John-John, saluting his father's casket after his funeral—truly gripping and sad moments. No public event that I have personally witnessed in my life can compare to the somber silence, sorrow, sadness, numbness, respect and reverence of that weekend.

Monday, 25 November, had been declared a national day of mourning by JFK's Vice-President and, in succession, President Lyndon B. Johnson. The funeral procession moved from the Capitol to the White House to St. Matthew's Cathedral and to Arlington National Cemetery where Kennedy was buried, his plot marked by an eternal flame. Millions of Americans watched the solemn, dignified and historic event on their black and white televisions.

To me, America was never the same after that, after the assassination of President Kennedy. Maybe it's because I was an impressionable young teenager, quite innocent and naïve as to the ways of the world. Still, that was the weekend America's innocence died, a country changed forever.

JFK—ASSASSINATION DATE NUMBERS

John Fitzgerald Kennedy was assassinated Friday, 22 November 1963. This is a very powerful day numerologically and there are correlations between it and John Kennedy's chart (following). Note the master number triangle formed by the day, month, 1st Pinnacle and 1st Challenge—all of which form a 77-14-5, a numerical pattern of loss.

Also of significance is the number 33 forming a tristack of the name "Kennedy," the 1st Pinnacle of the 22nd of November and JFK's Grand Challenge of a 7/33-6. Perhaps more noticeable is the hexstack of 7 energy associated with his assassination. As we've discussed, 7 is JFK's Lifepath—the lifepath housing the greatest potential for suffering, sorrow, tragedy, betrayal and tears.

(Next page)

Richard Andrew King

KENNEDY ASSASSINATION
DATE & NOTES
22 November 1963

1st
Pinnacle
33

1st
Epoch
22
Day

2nd
Epoch
11
Mo. Nov.

11
1st
Challenge

Notes

The four master numbers involved on the day of Kennedy's assassination total a 77-14-5 (tragedy and loss)

33 + 22 + 11 + 11 = 77

This intensifies the hexstack of 7 energy noted in the right column

77 reduces to a 14-5, the number of loss

A. "Kennedy" is a 33

B. 1st Pinnacle of the assassination date is a 33

C. JFK's Grand Challenge (the time of his death) is a 7/33-6

*This creates a 33 tristack

D. JFK'S Lifepath is a 7

E. Name Timeline PE of "Fitzgerald" (at death) was an 88-16-7

F. Letter Timeline at death in the "G" of "Fitzgerald" was a 7/5

G. Universal date at death (22 November 1963) reduces to a 7

H. "Dealey" (Plaza) where JFK was killed is a 7

I. JKF was buried on the 25th, a 7 calendar day

*This creates a 7 hexstack

F. JFK's funeral was on 25 November 1963, a 55-1 universal day matching his Crown Pinnacle 55-1 PE

SUMMARY

John Fitzgerald Kennedy was a juxtaposition of all that is noble and problematic in a leader. He had great charisma, charm, personal power. He was loved by many people, but as history would later discover, his personal involvements outside his marriage were a tarnish to his legacy. JFK's presidency was a true challenge, especially given the enormous changes in the global environment and the pressures intrinsic to them, such as the space race, the Civil Rights movement in America and the Cold War.

Kennedy's presidency, too, was a time of hope, courage, inspiration and a fairytale of Camelot. Sadly, it was also a time of great tragedy, tears, fears and suffering. How long-term history will judge JFK remains to be seen, but it was an unforgettable time with extreme highs and lows.

Some of the interesting components in The King's Numerology^{tm} chart of John Fitzgerald Kennedy are . . .

- The hepset (seven) of the master number 11
- The quintset (five) of the master number 33
- The 7/33-6 IR set in his 1st Pinnacle; 3rd and 4th Challenges
- The 7-8-6 Basic Matrix Umbrella (Lifepath, Expression, PE)
- His 55-1 Crown Pinnacle PE
- His Grand Challenge IR sets: 1/9, 11-2/1 and 7/33-6
- The numbers 33 and 7 associated with his assassination
- His funeral date of 25 November 1963, a 55-1, matching his Crown Pinnacle 55-1 PE

Richard Andrew King

JOHN F. KENNEDY – QUOTES

My fellow Americans, ask not what your country can do for you; ask what you can do for your country.

If anyone is crazy enough to want to kill a president of the United States, he can do it. All he must be prepared to do is give his life for the President's.

Let every nation know, whether it wishes us well or ill, that we shall pay any price, bear any burden, meet any hardship, support any friend, oppose any foe to assure the survival and the success of liberty.

It is an unfortunate fact that we can secure peace only by preparing for war.

In a very real sense, it will not be one man going to the moon, it will be an entire nation, for all of us must work to put him there.

Mankind must put an end to war before war puts an end to mankind.

Let us never negotiate out of fear, but let us never fear to negotiate.

Once you say you're going to settle for second, that's what happens to you in life.

Our growing softness, our increasing lack of physical fitness, is a menace to our security.

Change is the law of life, and those who look only to the past or present are certain to miss the future.

Conformity is the jailer of freedom and the enemy of growth.

The problems of the world cannot possibly be solved by skeptics or cynics whose horizons are limited by the obvious realities. We need men who can dream of things that never were.

Efforts and courage are not enough without purpose and direction.

Those who dare to fail miserably can achieve greatly.

Forgive your enemies, but never forget their names.

Those who make peaceful revolution impossible will make violent revolution inevitable.

Do not pray for easy lives. Pray to be stronger men.

As we express our gratitude, we must never forget that the highest appreciation is not to utter words, but to live by them.

Physical fitness is not only one of the most important keys to a healthy body, it is the basis of dynamic and creative intellectual activity.

The best road to progress is freedom's road.

The cost of freedom is always high, but Americans have always paid it. And one path we shall never choose, and that is the path of surrender, or submission.

Richard Andrew King

HISTORIC ICON #7

MARILYN MONROE

Born: Norma Jeane Mortenson – 1 June 1926

Died – 5 August 1962 (suspicious circumstances), age 36

----

* Legendary American Actress and Iconic Blonde Bombshell

* Cover girl—1st Issue of *Playboy*, December 1953 (Wikipedia)

(Photo courtesy of Weblo.com)

I want to be a big star more than anything.

It's something precious.

~ Marilyn Monroe

Richard Andrew King

In a world of notoriety, some people become famous, some rise to super-stardom, others transcend their celebrity to become icons. However, it is a rare few who become institutions. Marilyn Monroe is a global institution.

Born Norma Jeane Mortenson on 1 June 1926 in Los Angeles, California, to Gladys Baker, a psychologically distressed mother who was later committed to a health care facility, and a father who abandoned her, Marilyn Monroe spent much of her youth in foster homes and orphanages. Norma Jeane received the surname Baker at her baptismal but legally changed her name to Marilyn Monroe in 1956. 'Marilyn' was derived from the first name of stage actress Marilyn Miller and 'Monroe' from her mother's maiden name.

Arguably, during the 20th Century Marilyn Monroe was the most famous star of the silver screen. She exuded a blend of vulnerability, innocence, glamour and blonde-bombshell sensuality that hypnotized and captivated the modern world. A photographer named David Conover discovered her in 1944 while she was working in a factory inspecting parachutes to support the war effort.

In reflection of her inmost desires to be a big star, Monroe did not betray her dreams. She was a natural in front of the camera, and with a successful modeling career in ascendance she landed a studio contract in 1946 with 20th Century Fox. Soon thereafter, she divorced her first husband, Jimmy Dougherty, whom she had married four years earlier, dyed her hair blonde, changed her name to Marilyn Monroe and, just like that, presto poof, a legend-in-the-making was born. It's the stuff dreams and fairy tales are made of.

And a legend she was to become too. Of her thirty movies, the first was *The Shocking Miss Pilgrim* in 1947. She had a bit part and continued to play small parts until 1950 when she appeared in John Huston's thriller, *The Asphalt Jungle*. That same year she appeared in *All About Eve* which starred film great Bette Davis.

It was Monroe's performance as Rose Loomis in *Niagara* in 1953 that delivered her to stardom. Following would come lead roles in *Gentlemen Prefer Blondes,* which co-starred Jane Russell, and *How to Marry a Millionaire*, which featured film giants Lauren Bacall and Betty Grable.

In 1953 at the age of 27, she was voted Best New Actress by Photoplay Magazine. She went on to star in many more movies including *Bus Stop*, *The Prince and the Showgirl* and *Some Like It Hot* for which she won a Golden Globe for Best Actress in a Comedy.

Aside from being a famous actress, Monroe married famous baseball great Joe DiMaggio in 1954. Her second marriage, it unfortunately didn't even survive the first year. Her sexual image and their conflicting careers were major contributing factors to their split. Monroe and DiMaggio were divorced on 27 October 1954, just nine months after they had wed, though they did remain friends.

It was not long before Monroe married a third time. She and playwright Arthur Miller wed on 29 June 1956. He created the part of Roslyn Taber for her in the 1961 movie, *The Misfits*. It was to be her last movie. Likewise, her marriage to Miller would also be her last. The couple divorced on 20 January 1961, four and a half years after their marriage nuptials. Although Monroe's success at long-term marriage was decidedly dismal, her personal magnetism and professional success were not. At the Golden Globes the following year (1962) she was named female World Film Favorite.

Although living a famous public life of glitter and glamour, Monroe's personal life was steeped in pain, personal insecurity, instability, mystery and tragedy. Her own quotes give a sense of her personal battles and turmoils. Voluptuous and desirable, she was alleged to have had affairs with President of the United States John F. Kennedy, his brother Robert Kennedy (Attorney General of the United States), as well as other famous men, among whom were Marlon Brando, Frank Sinatra and Elia Kazan. The key word, of course, is alleged—more mystery to the Monroe mystique.

Relationships played a pivotal role throughout Monroe's life but by her own indirect admission they did not help create a strong foundation for her.

> *My work is the only ground I've ever had to stand on. I seem to have a whole superstructure with no foundation – but I'm working on the foundation.*

Richard Andrew King

Was Marilyn Monroe, in essence, a beautiful but fragile damsel in distress looking for the masculine love she never knew; perhaps the father she never had? Would her life have been more stable had she been raised by devoted, nurturing, compassionate parents? Perhaps. However, her destiny did not avail her of such a fate. Interestingly, her life was somewhat like that of Princess Diana of Wales who would follow her into a very similar destiny. Both were beautiful women in search of love. They each had unhappy childhoods, fame beyond belief, multiple romantic heartaches, marriages to famous men, adoration from the multitudes, paparazzi pressure beyond compare, mysterious liaisons, tragic deaths, short lives and legacies of renown reserved only for incandescent heroines. Hauntingly, they both lived in the limelight for sixteen years. Monroe's first studio contract occurred in August of 1946 with 20th Century Fox. She died in August of 1962. Diana married Prince Charles in July of 1981 and died in August of 1997. Furthermore, they shared the same numerological Umbrella: 7 Lifepath, 4 Expression, 2 PE!

Marilyn's famously fabled life ended like a Shakespearean tragedy. On 5 August 1962, her lifeless body was found at her home in Brentwood, California. She had apparently died in her sleep, victim of a drug overdose. But was the overdose intentionally self-inflicted, giving thought to the idea of suicide? Was it an accidental overdose? Was it inflicted by someone else? Was Marilyn Monroe, in fact, murdered? There is much speculation as to the latter. The controversy of such a homicide has not been quieted to this day. Still, her death is a mystery, much like the mystery involved in the assassination of JFK just 15 months later on 22 November 1963.

There is no doubt Marilyn Monroe was bigger than life, the quintessential blonde whose gorgeous face, figure and siren-like seductive persona mesmerized the masses. She was more than a common star, more than a super-star. She was a goddess of film and fantasy, a veritable cinematic seductress whose fame and flame would forever light the halls and walls of 20th Century celebrity.

Still, however, Marilyn Monroe was a common soul and, like many of us, somewhat lost and sadly in need of the love and nurturing she never found. Although her memory and magic still mesmerize people today, one is given to ponder the true power of personality that she possessed—this common ordinary little girl with a dream to become a star, who transcended super-stardom and, in a relatively short professional life of sixteen years, became, not just a movie legend, but a veritable cinematic institution.

PROVOCATIVE QUESTIONS

- What numbers played a major role in Monroe's siren-esque persona?
- What two master numbers drove Monroe's sex symbol image?
- What numbers reveal Monroe's difficult early life?
- What master numbers drove Monroe's success and stardom?
- What three voids played a part in Monroe's dramatic life?
- Which void was responsible for her image issues—positive and negative?
- What numbers reflect her mental problems and bouts of depression?
- What was Marilyn's numeric connection to the Kennedys?
- Why were Marilyn's marriages doomed from the beginning?
- What is significant about the numbers at the time of her death?

MARILYN MONROE – NUMBERS OF A SEX SIREN

More than anything else, Marilyn Monroe was known for her sex-siren persona. She was pursued by some of the most famous men of her time who came from all walks of life—politics, sports, theater, music, cinema, publishing. She also, no doubt, filled the imaginations and reveries of millions of men the world over. What numbers in Monroe's chart reveal such a powerful and magnetic hypersexual persona? There are three:

- the master number 33-6
- the master number 66-3
- the number 5

One of the amazing components of Monroe's chart is the amount of internal stacking of the master number 33. Her Material Soul contains a tristack of this powerfully expressive sexual energy, an energy which can also lead to severe addictions because of its pleasure-seeking quality. Having one set of 33 energy is powerful, but three is extremely rare. This internal tristack of 33 energy can be

Richard Andrew King

written as 33-6^3, or perhaps a more visual depiction would be 33-33-33 which, when combined, creates a 99, the master number of universal power and rulership. Because the Material Soul rules one's worldly needs, wants and desires, it was at the core of Monroe's motivations. She wanted, if not craved, to be a sex symbol.

To add more nuclear power to this 33 Material Soul, her middle name of "Jeane" maintains a Name Timeline PE of yet another 33-6 tristack! This was active between ages 26 to 42, the period in which she died. These dual 33-6 tristacks are visible in the following grids of her Basic Matrix and Name Timeline.

Basic Matrix: Norma Jeane Mortenson (Marilyn Monroe)

LP	Exp.	PE	Soul	MS	Nature	MN	Voids
7	22-4	11-2	8	33-6^3	5	66-3	3-7-8

Name Timeline (NTL): Norma Jeane Mortenson

		First	Middle	Last
	Names	Norma	Jeane	Mortenson
	Timeline	birth to 25	26 to 42	43 to 85
	General	25	17	43
	IR Set	7v	8v	7v
		5	6	5
	Master #s		33-6^3	
			Dies here at 36	

Adding to the double 33-6 tristack is the 66-3 in her Material Nature (see the Basic Matrix above). This is also a powerfully sex-charged master number. It is not as common as the 33 but it is nonetheless powerful.

The third number creating Monroe's sexual persona is the number 5. It rules the five senses, variety, diversity, stimulation, experience, freedom and exploration. Together, the single numbers 5 and 6 are the most potent sexual combination. Monroe's Nature was a 5. She loved variety. Hence, her many lovers. One man was simply not enough for her. Basically, Marilyn Monroe could be described as sex incarnate. Her inmost desires, personality and life manifested her enchantress image.

Unfortunately, such massive pleasure-dominated and self-expressive energy has a downside or more precisely, a dark side. Marilyn's addictions to drugs and alcohol, not just men, were a fatal flaw in her life. Too, and a fact that cannot be ignored, is that the number 3 was void in Marilyn's chart. There was not a C, L or U in her natal name of Norma Jeane Mortenson, creating a potentially disastrous (and sadly realized) effect not only in the field of sexuality and drug use, but in the fields of image, health and beauty. The twelve 3s of her dual 33^3 voided dyads can be numerically depicted as:

The Twelve 3s Forming Monroe's Dual 33 Triset

3v3v	3v3v	3v3v	3v3v	3v3v	3v3v
Set #1	Set #2	Set #3	Set #4	Set #5	Set #6

Therefore, even though there was extreme power in her 33^3 Material Soul and her 33^3 Name Timeline PE of 'Jeane,' it was unbridled power, not unlike a runaway horse with no bridle. Arguably, the very numbers that created Marilyn Monroe's famous sexual persona and prowess also were instrumental in her no less famous, mysterious and highly suspicious demise.

PROBLEMATIC EARLY LIFE

It is heart-wrenching to read accounts of Marilyn Monroe's early life. It's one thing to change homes frequently, but families and multiple foster homes? And to have no father and a psychiatrically ill mother? How extremely difficult is this on a child? And were such adversities, which are visible in both Monroe's Life Matrix and her Name Timeline of "Norma," responsible for her image, sex, drugs and male issues in her life?

Richard Andrew King

1st Epoch-Pinnacle-Challenge Period

The many changes in Monroe's home life are revealed in her 5/9 1st Challenge. The absentee/abandonment father issues are visible in her 1/5 1st Epoch and the problems, especially mental problems, of her mother are indicated in her 1st Pinnacle of 7v/11-2.

1st Epoch-Pinnacle-Challenge Period
Voids: 3-7-8
Norma Jeane Mortenson: 1 June 1926

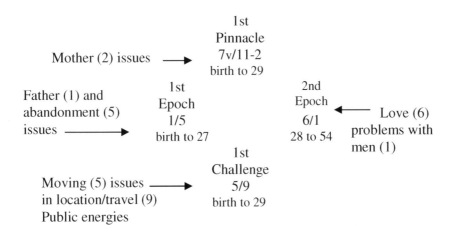

Name Timeline of "Norma"

Marilyn's first birth name of "Norma" carries a 7v/5 IR set. Once again, the 7 void and its turbulence presents its challenges as another energetic piece in the puzzle of Monroe's life. This 7v/5 Influence/Reality set is created by taking the 7 of the name "Norma" and funneling or filtering it (by addition) through her 7 Lifepath, which is also void due to the lack of a G, P, or Y in her birth name, to create a 5 in reduction (7 + 7 = 14: 1 + 4 = 5). The 7 is a very lonely number, an internal energy that can create turmoil, tumult, tears, sadness, sorrow and tragedy. On its positive side, it can also create great awareness, substance and spirituality. As the famous American-Lebanese artist, writer and poet, Khalil Gibran, beautifully wrote:

> *Out of suffering have emerged the strongest souls;*
> *the most massive characters are seared with scars.*

Therefore, the dominant IR sets during the first phase of Marilyn Monroe's life were the 7v/5 NTL, the 7v/11-2 1st Pinnacle, 1/5 1st Epoch and 5/9 1st Challenge. Combined, they reflect an accurate landscape of the early journey of Monroe's 7 Lifepath, itself a path of spiritual challenges, tears, sorrow and potential tragedy.

SUCCESS AND STARDOM

Although there was a massive amount of sexual energy in Monroe's chart, sexual energy alone won't send someone into the skies of success and stardom. There has to be more. In Monroe's case, one of the major number patterns corroborating such success was her 22-4/44-8 master IR set which occupied her 3rd/Grand Pinnacle, the core of her 7 Lifepath.

So far in our review of the featured individuals in this work we've seen the powerful effect of both the 22 and the 44. They are potent master numbers of power, wealth, work, service, connection, interaction and involvement. But in most cases to this point the 22 and 44 were separate and not conjoined. In Monroe's case, these separate master numbers combined to form the extremely dynamic 22-4/44-8 Influence/Reality dyad. This is arguably the strongest indicator of Monroe's success, stardom and fame. Yes, there are other numbers in her chart, but to have such a forceful master pair in the center of her life cannot be overlooked.

Coinciding with the timeline of Monroe's 3rd/Grand Pinnacle is her 3rd/Grand Challenge which houses two IR sets, the 2/6 and 7v/11-2. Once again the 7v/11-2 energy looms large, but in this case it references Marilyn's problems both with herself and her relationships. As we recall, the 7v/11-2 dyad occupies Monroe's 1st Pinnacle and early life in which she had problems with her mother. Regardless of the players, the 7v/11-2 pattern potenially indicates problems, concerns, difficulties and troubles (7v) in the field of relationship (2), whether the relationship is with the self or others. The 11-2 can also indicate the treacheries and deceits of others.

The other IR set in Monroe's Grand Challenge is a 2/6. Here again is the circumstance of relationship, others and female energy (2) playing itself out in the arena of the heart, home, love, romance, compassion and nurturing (6).

Richard Andrew King

LIFE MATRIX
Voids: 3-7-8
NORMA JEANE MORTENSON
(Marilyn Monroe)
1 JUNE 1926

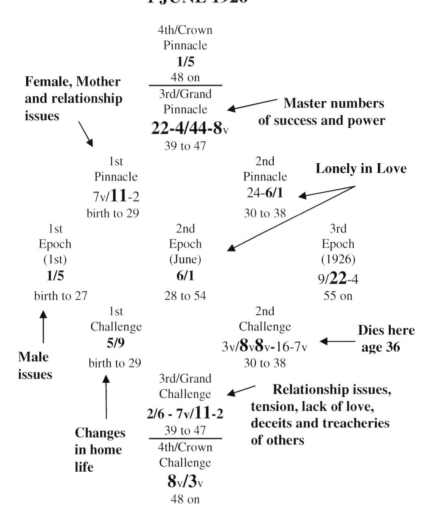

4th/Crown
Pinnacle
1/5
48 on
_____
3rd/Grand
Pinnacle
22-4/44-8v
39 to 47

**Master numbers
of success and power**

**Female, Mother
and relationship
issues**

1st
Pinnacle
7v/**11**-2
birth to 29

2nd
Pinnacle
24-**6/1**
30 to 38

Lonely in Love

1st
Epoch
(1st)
1/5
birth to 27

2nd
Epoch
(June)
6/1
28 to 54

3rd
Epoch
(1926)
9/22-4
55 on

1st
Challenge
5/9
birth to 29

2nd
Challenge
3v/**8**v**8**v-16-7v
30 to 38

**Dies here
age 36**

**Male
issues**

**Changes
in home
life**

3rd/Grand
Challenge
2/6 - 7v/**11**-2
39 to 47
_____
4th/Crown
Challenge
8v/**3**v
48 on

**Relationship issues,
tension, lack of love,
deceits and treacheries
of others**

TRAGIC LIFE AND VOIDS

As we've discussed, voids can create problems in people's lives, and Marilyn's voids certainly played a major role in her sorrows and sufferings.

Monroe had three voids in her birth name of Norma Jeane Mortenson. These were the 3 (no C-L or U), the 7 (no G-P or Y) and the 8 (no H-Q or Z).

The 3 rules image, health, beauty, children, sex, pleasure and communication. The abundance of 3 energy in her chart vis-à-vis the master number 33 had a major impact on her beauty, talent, sexuality and magnetic public image, but the fact that the 3 was void gave a negative spin to her life. Her addictions to drugs, alcohol and men; her lack of children, her health issues—all were impacted by the 3 void.

People often crave what they don't have and therefore they seek what they don't have in ways often not conducive to their overall well-being. Monroe's statement, *I want to be a big star more than anything. It's something precious*, reveals much about her lack of a positive self image.

The number 7 addresses wisdom, thought, reflection, introspection, solitude, recession, withdrawal and mental wholeness. One of the major observations of the 7 void is that it can manifest as mental stress, depression, indiscretion, a lack of substance, wisdom, inner strength and the inability to handle the pressures of life. If one confronts these issues head on, the void can be filled, but if one tries to run away from them, avoid them, or attempt to drown them in a sea of alcohol, drugs, sexual liaisons, etc., the problems only become worse. People can be very smart with a 7 void (and Monroe had a high IQ) but equally foolish and hollow at the same time. This 7 void played a major role in Monroe's mental instability, drug issues, feelings of loneliness and isolation, as well as the problems and chaos surrounding her mother and close personal relationships.

The number 8 governs interaction, involvement, management, flow, orchestration, connection and punctuality. When voided in a chart, the 8 can manifest as mismanagement, disconnection and disruption where things don't flow smoothly or consistently and being tardy—a trait for which

Richard Andrew King

Monroe was well known. Basically, with an 8 void there's a break in the concept of coordination, flow and an understanding of what has to be done to keep things connected and running smoothly.

When we take a simple cursory look at Monroe's numbers, as well as the difficult periods of her life vis-à-vis her Life Matrix and Name Timelines, we see how her voids all played major roles—from her relationship issues in the 7v/11-2 IR set, to her health problems in her 3v/7v and 8v/3v dyads, to her fame and fortune through the 4/8v IR set and her death in the 3v/7v 2nd Challenge. The bottom line with voids is that they create potential problems in people's lives, problems which need to be addressed through acting on the positive aspect of the numbers involved in order to balance the negative effects they can create.

MONROE-KENNEDY CONNECTION

The connection between Marilyn Monroe and the Kennedys couldn't be more clear. The name "Kennedy" is a 33 vibration with a 6 crown addcap! Need more be said? And as we've discussed, Monroe has a massive amount of 33 energy in her numerology chart—all of which is voided! How could there not be problems between them.

It is worth noting that Marilyn's NTL of "Jeane" carries an 8v/6 IR set. Clearly, this is a disconnect (8v) with the 6—the single cipher of love, lust, family, matters of the heart, as well as the name "Kennedy."

What is also fascinating is that Norma Jeane Mortenson's stage surname of "Monroe" is also an 8, creating another layer of complexity to her life through stacking and thus intensifying the 8v/6 in her life. Therefore, the "Monroe/Kennedy" connection is revealed in the 8v/6 IR set (the 8 of "Monroe" and the 6 of "Kennedy").

Interestingly, it was during this 8v/6 NTL of "Jeane" (with its numeric sibling, "Monroe") that Monroe died under very suspicious circumstances. Happenstance?

DOOMED MARRIAGES

In addition to her many relationships, Marilyn Monroe had three marriages:

1. James Dougherty (1942 to 1946; she married at age 16)
2. Joe DiMaggio (1954 to 1954; she married at age 27)
3. Arthur Miller (1956 to 1961; she married at age 30)

Why were these marriages doomed from the beginning? Was it simply because during her marriages her numbers never supported a lasting or comparatively problem-free relationship? Marilyn's first marriage to James Dougherty was in 1942 when she was 16 years old during her Name Timeline of "Norma" from birth (1926) to age 25 (1951). Its IR set was a 7v/5. This portends trouble (7) resulting in loss and changes (5).

Running concurrently with her NTL of "Norma" and creating another problematic layer of energy was her 1st Pinnacle (from birth to age 29), which carried a 7v/11-2 IR set, reinforcing the trouble (7) in relationships (11-2).

Monroe's 5/9 1st Challenge of changes (5) and endings (9), as well as her 1st Epoch of a 1/5 indicating abandonment of male energy simply added more fuel to a fire that could not be extinguished.

Marilyn's second marriage to Joe DiMaggio was in 1954 when she was 27. She was still in the timeframe of her 1st Pinnacle/Challenge couplet of 7v/11-2 and 5/9 respectively. Plus, she entered her second Name Timeline of "Jeane" at age 26 which housed an 8v/6 IR set showing a disconnection (8 void) in love (6). It's virtually impossible to keep anything together on a permanent basis when the 8 is voided in a chart.

Monroe's third marriage to Arthur Miller when she was 30 was still in the 8v/6 NTL of "Jeane." Plus, her 2nd Challenge was 3v/7v indicating more problems and sorrow (7v) in her happiness, joy and health (3v). Her 2nd Pinnacle was a 6/1 which can reference being solo (1) in love (6). Basically, there was simply too much composite negatively-charged relationship energy for

Richard Andrew King

Monroe to have a successful marriage. Even had she lived, her 1/5, 7v/11-2, 8v/3v and 7v/5 IR sets would have prevented her from experiencing an enduring relationship. It must be remembered also that Monroe's 7 Lifepath carried with it the potential for problems in her love life for the entirety of her life from the moment of birth, just like that of Princess Diana and her 7 Lifepath.

NUMBERS AT DEATH

The numbers in Monroe's chart at the time of her death were extremely reflective of a life falling apart, the most portentous number pattern being the 3v/7v IR set in her 2nd Challenge where the 3 void references negative aspects of life, health and well-being, and the 7 void references trouble, stress, turmoil and tribulation. Plus, the 3v/7v IR set houses an 88 root to the 7, creating an IR set that can be viewed as 3v/8v8v-7v. Notice that all the numbers are voided, making the timeframe of Monroe's life from 30 to 38 extremely difficult, turbulent and . . . as history has proven, fatal. Exacerbating the 3v/7v IR set in Monroe's 2nd Challenge is her 5/3v IR set in her Letter Timeline. Marilyn died at age 36 in the "N" of "Jeane." This 5/3v IR set originating from the "N" (the 14th letter of the alphabet) references loss and detachment (14-5) of life and well-being (3v).

These IR sets, plus the enormous amount of 3 voided energy in her chart, could not have boded well for Monroe. Overall, she was born into a destiny that was difficult, challenging and unfortunately tragic in spite of her great success and fame.

Marilyn Monroe wanted to be a big star. Diana wanted to be a princess. They both got what they wanted, and what they got was a forlorn and tragic life. This should remind us all to be weary of what we wish for. Stardom and the limelight, however scintillating, promising and alluring, may well morph into the terrifying dark hole of midnight.

Marilyn Monroe

The Prince and the Showgirl, 1957

(Photo courtesy of Wikimedia Commons)

Richard Andrew King

MASTER NUMBERS IN MONROE'S CHART

	Master Numbers in Marilyn Monroe's Chart
11	Life Performance/Experience (PE)
	1st Pinnacle PE
	3rd Challenge (Grand) PE
22	Expression (birth name)
	Grand Pinnacle
	3rd (Grand) Epoch PE
33	*Internal Triset* in her Soul
	Internal Triset in her Name Timeline PE of "Jeane"
	[Note: both of these internal trisets are extremely rare]
44	3rd (Grand) Pinnacle PE
55	Material Nature of her stage name "Marilyn Monroe"
66	Material Nature
77	none
88	2nd Challenge PE
99	none

SUMMARY

Marilyn Monroe was a legend in her own time, a dynamic powerhouse who created an iconic image surviving decades. People are just as fascinated with her life today as they were in those thirty-six brief years of her very successful but tragedy-laden life. She was a platinum blonde bombshell with a platinum resume of universal appeal. There was no one like her before. There has been no one like her since, much like Elvis Presley and Princess Diana. She was uniquely destined to be one of the most memorable individuals of all time, not just in America, but in the world.

Some of the interesting components in the numerology chart of Marilyn Monroe are . . .

- The 7 void Lifepath

- The 1/5 1st Epoch, 7v/11-2 1st Pinnacle and 5/9 1st Challenge

- 33 *Internal Triset* in her Soul [very rare]

- 33 *Internal Triset* in her Name Timeline PE of "Jeane" [very rare]

- The 33 connection with the Kennedys

- The 22-4/44-8v Grand Pinnacle

- The 3-7-8 voids

- The 3v/8v8v-16-7v IR set in her 2nd Challenge when she died

- The 8v/3v Crown Challenge

- The many numeric connections with another fated heroine, Princess Diana

Richard Andrew King

MARILYN MONROE – QUOTES

I want to be a big star more than anything. It's something precious.

Hollywood's a place where they'll pay you a thousand dollars for a kiss and fifty cents for your soul.

An actress is not a machine, but they treat you like a machine, a money machine.

A sex symbol becomes a thing. I just hate to be a thing.

My work is the only ground I've ever had to stand on. I seem to have a whole superstructure with no foundation—but I'm working on the foundation.

Being a sex symbol is a heavy load to carry, especially when one is tired, hurt and bewildered.

Dreaming about being an actress is more exciting then being one.

(Cross reference with Diana's quote: *Being a princess isn't all it's cracked up to be.*)

First, I'm trying to prove to myself that I'm a person. Then maybe I'll convince myself that I'm an actress.

I am not interested in money. I just want to be wonderful.

I'm very definitely a woman and I enjoy it.

QUOTES About MARILYN MONROE

It is a disease of our profession that we believe a woman with physical appeal has no talent. Marilyn is as near a genius as any actress I ever knew. She is an artist beyond artistry. She is the most completely realized and authentic film actress since Garbo. She has that same unfathomable mysteriousness. She is pure cinema.

~ Joshua Logan - Director of Bus Stop

Marilyn had the power. She was the wind, that comet shape that Blake draws blowing around a sacred figure. She was the light, and the goddess, and the moon; the space and the dream, the mystery and the danger, but everything else all together, too, including Hollywood, and the girl next door that every guy wants to marry. ~ Bert Stern

... She gave more to the still camera than any actress...any woman...I've ever photographed. ~ Richard Avedon

Richard Andrew King

HISTORIC ICON #8

MICHAEL JACKSON

Born: Michael Joseph Jackson – 29 August 1958

Died – 25 June 2009, age 50

(by acute propofol intoxication)

----

* King of Pop (Self-Proclaimed)

* Best-Selling Album of All Time – *Thriller* (Wikipedia)

* Most Successful Entertainer of All Time (Guinness World Records)

(Photo courtesy of PublicDomainPictures.net)

Richard Andrew King

As Howard Hughes was the most famously mysterious and reclusive person of his time, Michael Jackson was the most famous and bizarre person of his. Both excelled at what they did. Their names are legend. Yet, they were both very troubled individuals whose eccentric behavior matched their exclusive genius and led them down a dark road of destructive egocentricity.

Michael Joseph Jackson was born on 29 August 1958 and died from acute propofol intoxication on 25 June 2009 according to the Los Angeles County Coroner. His emaciated body, covered with needle marks, scars, bruises and a practically bald, peach-fuzz head (which he had covered with a wig), had wasted away to seemingly bare skin and bones.

Jackson was a musical phenom. His accomplishments in the world of entertainment and music are unrivaled. Yet, it's also fair to say that his bizarre behavior and life are also unrivaled. Self-proclaimed or not, Michael Jackson's title as the "King of Pop" is deserved. By the same token, his title, "Wacko Jacko" is nonetheless deserved. Jackson was a brilliant artist and performer, and some would argue that he was not just strange but deranged, a characteristic not uncommon to other historic figures with great talent.

For example, what balanced, normal, whole, mature adult male dangles his baby over a balcony and has sleepovers with children in his bed? What can be said of a person who continually changes his appearance with multiple plastic surgeries, travels around with a chimpanzee, publically dons a black mask, sleeps in a hyperbaric chamber and wears pajamas to court? Is moon-walking on the roof of an SUV after being arraigned on criminal charges for child abuse reflective of a balanced mind? Is it not strange for an adult to build and live in a mansion named Neverland while living in a Peter Pan world full of toys, amusement rides and amenities, a train station, games, statues of children and a triple-locked secret closet within his master bedroom closet? Are these examples the manifestation of a balanced, healthy, whole, mature person, especially a grown man? There's absolutely no question Michael Jackson was a superlative performer. There's also no question he was superlatively bizarre.

Michael Jackson's destiny is so clear in his numbers that his life serves as an excellent example of study for students of numerology. Jackson led a famous but tragic life, a life both revered by some and reviled by others; a life which exemplified a meteoric rise to fame and fortune but an equally meteoric fall from grace into the depths of misfortune, despair and ignominy.

Michael Jackson was a self-proclaimed and narcissistic King of Pop suffering from a messiah complex who demanded the media refer to him in such terms. One has to wonder if he ever concluded that William Shakespeare, the acknowledged king of literary drama, was correct when he noted, *Uneasy lies the head that wears a crown* (Henry IV, Part 2 - Act 3, Scene 1).

Jackson's life also reflected the truism that the drop from a high place has fatal consequences, and that kings – self-proclaimed or not – are subject to the same divine laws as everyone else, that no one is exempt from *the* Law which operates like gravity and without regard to persons, however talented or famous. Laws create boundaries, boundaries which offer protection from without (as in worldly and societal laws) and within (as in spiritual laws). Worldly laws are arbitrary; spiritual laws are not.

PROVOCATIVE QUESTIONS

- What numbers reveal Jackson's musical genius, fame, egomania?
- Which numbers show his issues with children, family and image?
- What do the events of Jackson's hair catching on fire during a Pepsi commercial in 1984, his interview with Oprah in 1993 and his divorce from Debbie Rowe in 1999 have in common?
- What is extremely unique about Jackson's Challenges?
- What number pattern and linkage reveal his interest in children?
- What numbers reveal Jackson's rise and fall?
- What single number forms a quintstack at Jackson's death?

Richard Andrew King

MICHAEL JACKSON – BASIC MATRIX

Jackson's 33-6 and 66-3 master IR sets reveal powerful music numbers. Elvis Presley also had these master numbers in his Basic Matrix, although Jackson's Material Soul houses a 66-3^2 double stack. Is it coincidental that both the *King of Rock and Roll* and the *King of Pop* have these numbers in common? And let's not forget Marilyn Monroe. Her chart housed the 33 and 66, too.

Basic Matrix: Michael Joseph Jackson

LP	Exp.	PE	Soul	MS	Nature	MN	Voids
6	8	77-5	33-6	66-3^2	11-2	44-8^2	none

Jackson's 8 Expression and double stack of 44-8^2 in his Material Nature (MN) reveal a personality harmonizing with success, wealth, comfort, commercialism and interaction. His 6 Lifepath (LP) illustrates the family lessons which would dominate his life. The 77-5 PE supports an eccentric, shy, reclusive reality. The 11-2 Nature discloses a personality based in relationship. The numbers 2-6-8 together focus on others, love and connection respectively (next page).

LIFE MATRIX
Voids: none
MICHAEL JACKSON
29 AUGUST 1958

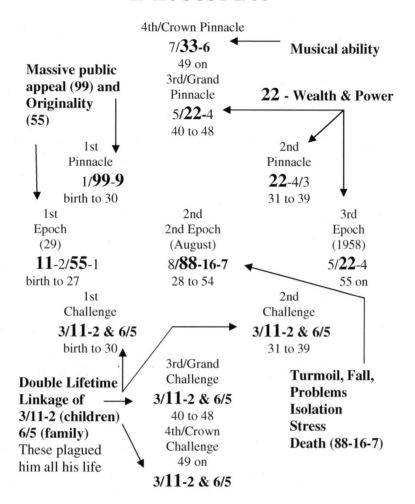

MUSICAL GENIUS, GLOBAL FAME & EGOMANIA

1st Epoch: 29-11-2/55-1: Birth to age 27

The period of Michael Jackson's life from birth to age 27, combined with his 1st PC Couplet from birth to age 30, was clearly the time of his life that housed his musical genius, fame, public consumption and revolutionary musical status. His 1st Epoch is a 29-11-2/55-1. The 11-2 illustrates

Richard Andrew King

his inspirational and personal vitality and energy in the realm of personal relationship, others and music. His 55-1 PE (the outcome of this inspirational 11-2 energy moving through his 8 Expression filter) reveals enormous change, movement, originality, pioneering, action and new direction. Jackson has been rightly extolled as a music revolutionary and true original, being the first Black artist to appear on MTV. His videos, music and dance moves, especially in his history-setting album *Thriller*, exemplify this unique and original 55-1 status. What is interesting is that Jackson named himself the "King of Pop" which itself is a 55-1 vibration, matching the 55-1 PE in his 1st Epoch! This is far too coincidental to be accidental, further averring the invisible truth of numbers and numerology as a science. The underlying 29 energy (originating from the day of his birth) shows power (9) in the realm of relationship and others (2). This is an intense and dominating energy.

1st Pinnacle: 1/99-9: Birth to age 30

It's impossible to get any more iconic and famous than this 1/99 combination. The 1/9 cipher lives in the public eye. The 1 represents the self, the ego, the originator, doer, activator, leader and star. The 99 represents the masses, public acclaim, popularity and recognition. The symbol for the 9 is the crown. More than any combination, it is this 1/99-9 combination that rocketed Michael Jackson to global stardom. Elvis Presley did not have this specifically in his chart, but he did have 1s and 9s dominant, as well as a 99-9 PE. No two numbers acting in concert have more potential for creating individual power and fame than the 1 and 9. Together they represent the star (the one who is the center of attention) and the crown (the symbol of rulership holding magnetic power over the masses).

As positive as this 1/99-9 combination was for Jackson, it was also immensely instrumental in his destruction. This combination represents the ego and its power, and if that ego and power are not controlled and placed in the proper perspective, they possess the ability to inflate a person's sense of self-worth to levels of extreme egomania, self-absorption and narcissistic self-proclamation, placing him or her on a pedestal in a tower of enormous height, an edifice insuring a fall of gigantic proportions. This type of human expression is sadly common in the world of celebrity and flies in the face of all that is spiritually appropriate and divine.

Egomania

It is no secret that Jackson's ego was highly inflated and beyond mitigation, this in stark contrast to his seemingly soft and tender nature. It was Jackson himself, not the public, who coined himself the "King of Pop" and demanded, not asked according to one reporter, that the media do the same. It was Jackson who, saturated with a Messiah Complex as reported by Chris Ayers in a Times Online article, commissioned a giant replica of *The Last Supper* by famed artist Leonardo da Vinci to hang above his bed. In the modern day portrait by Nate Giorgio (nategiorgio.com), Jackson, adorned with a gold-laced coat, placed himself as Christ in the center of the table and replaced Christ's disciples with famous people—Abraham Lincoln, John F. Kennedy, Thomas Edison, Albert Einstein, Walt Disney, Charlie Chaplin, Elvis Presley and Little Richard.

Artwork: *Heroes – The Last Supper* by Nate Giorgio (nategiorgio.com). Photo courtesy of Google images

For all his worldly and temporal notoriety, did Jackson actually believe himself to be a messiah and divinely superior to these esteemed individuals, except perhaps for the entertainers? What humble person would ever think of doing such a thing, let alone doing it? Does it not stagger the imagination to understand the dimensions of such an ego, an ego that would replace itself as Christ in the *Last Supper*—one of the most sacred paintings of all time? This behavior certainly brings into focus three germane Biblical quotes:

Richard Andrew King

1. *Be not deceived; God is not mocked: for whatsoever a man soweth, that shall he also reap.* (Galatians 6:7)

2. *Pride goeth before destruction and an haughty spirit before a fall.* (Proverbs 16:18)

3. *Better it is to be of an humble spirit with the lowly, than to divide the spoil with the proud.* (Proverbs 16:19)

PROBLEMATIC CHALLENGE ISSUES: CHILDREN, FAMILY, IMAGE

Michael Jackson was challenged his entire life with issues related to his childhood, children, family and personal image. He was often heard remarking that he had no childhood because he was always working and that his father was very hard on him and his siblings. These issues are revealed in his Life Matrix in a double lifetime linkage from birth to death in the IR sets 3/2 and 6/5. Children are ruled by the number 3; relationships by the number 2; families by the number 6; changes, loss, versatility by the number 5. The number 3 also rules pleasure, joy, communication, personal image and sex—all areas in which Jackson was challenged during his life. The number 6 also represents music, as it is one of the components in the artistic triad 3-6-9. The 5 PE stemming from this 6 certainly helped give Jackson a diversity of ability in the music field.

It is rare to have lifetime linkage. Several of the featured individuals in this work have it—General George Patton, Howard Hughes, Oprah Winfrey and Sarah Palin in particular. Howard Hughes had two sets of lifetime linkage—the 3/1 and 9/7. However, they were present in different components of his Life Matrix. Michael Jackson is the only one of our featured icons who had a double lifetime linkage in all four of his Challenges. This is extremely rare, and the dual power of his 3/2 and 6/5 Challenge IR sets contributed to his life's problems. Most people's charts have different Challenges throughout the life, thus creating a variation of issues to manage. Because Michael Jackson's four dual Challenges were all the same throughout his life, there was no change and, hence, greater intensity in their manifestation.

The 3/2 Challenge played a major role in Jackson's alleged child molestation issues and his lifelong attraction to a childlike life, as witnessed by his estate of Neverland and its Peter Pan fairytale ambiance.

The number 3 also rules health, beauty and image. It was the 3 in his life linkage Challenges that contributed to Jackson's mutilation of himself, his many plastic surgeries to change his face, as well as his drug issues. In effect, he was constantly challenged by his own self-image. He simply wasn't happy with the way he looked. All of Jackson's 3 energy reinforced his narcissism and vanity, giving rise to his bizarre appearance as he grew older. Sadly, a once good-looking young man continued to look more and more bizarre to the public, prompting the press to dub him "Wacko Jacko."

PEPSI HAIR BURNING, OPRAH INTERVIEW, ROWE DIVORCE

The truth of numbers as reflected in Michael Jackson's life is also quite apparent in three dramatic incidents of his life, all of which have a synchronized numerical bond:

1. Michael's hair catching on fire during a Pepsi commercial shoot on 27 January 1984, age 25
2. His interview with Oprah Winfrey on 10 February 1993, age 34
3. His divorce from Debbie Rowe on 8 October 1999, age 41

The common bond linking these three incidents is that they all occurred during a 1/7 natal Letter Timeline period illustrating the self (1) in stress, distress, concern or examination (7). The hair-burning incident was in the "A" of *Michael* at age 25; the interview with Winfrey was in the "J" of *Joseph* at age 34; the divorce from Debbie Rowe was in the "S" of *Joseph* at age 41.

Name	M	I	C	H	A	E	L	J	O	S	E	P
Timeline	0-4	5-13	14-16	17-24	25	26-30	31-33	34	35-40	41	42-46	47-53
I/R Sets	4	9	3	8	1	5	3	1	6	1	5	7
	1	6	9	5	7	2	9	7	3	7	2	4

1/7 IR Sets of Numeric Synchronicity

Richard Andrew King

BEGINNING OF THE FALL

As was stated earlier, Jackson's life is clearly visible in his numbers. His Life Matrix reveals his fame, celebrity, power and uniqueness. His Name Timeline corroborates his decline and ultimate collapse.

Name Timeline (NTL): Michael Joseph Jackson			
	First	Middle	Last
Names	Michael	Joseph	Jackson
Timeline	birth to 33	34 to 61	62 to 80
Years	33	28	19
IR Sets	6	1	1
	3	7 ← →	7
Master #s	33	88-16-7	
		Dies here at 50	

In Jackson's NTL above, notice the change of IR sets from his first name of *Michael* to his second name of *Joseph* and then to *Jackson*. The name *Michael* was active from birth through age 33 and housed a 33 master number as part of a 6/3 IR set, which we know is artistically powerful.

When Jackson was 34 years of age, his IR set changed to a 1/7 in general terms but a 1/88-16-7 in specific terms when he moved into the NTL of *Joseph*. This 1/88-16-7 IR set portends trouble, turmoil, tumult, tragedy, tears, angst, heartbreak and heartache. It is not a number pattern of happiness. It is a pattern of spiritual testing and purification, often portending a fall in disgrace and ignominy. This 1/7 IR set was active from age 34 through the end of his *Jackson* NTL which lasted through age 80. Therefore, Michael's life would not have been pleasant had he lived. His numbers divulge a journey in which he (1) would have been in constant turmoil (7) from age 34 to 80. Had he lived to age 81, his NTL would have recycled to his first name of *Michael* and its 6/3 IR set.

Compounding Jackson's 1/7 Name Timeline is that at age 34 when he moved into his *Joseph* NTL, he also simultaneously entered the Letter Timeline "J" of *Joseph* which also reflects a 1/7 energy. Additionally, we see in his Life Matrix that at this time of his life he was already living through his 8/88-16-7 2nd Epoch. These three energies created a tristack of powerful problematic energy when he was 34 in his natal year (Jackson turned 34 on 29 August 1992).

And what happened when he was 34? In early August of 1993, just weeks before his 35th birthday, Jackson became the subject of a criminal investigation for sexual child abuse by the Los Angeles Police Department. This was the exact time when he entered his 1/7 NTL and 1/7 LTL which was encased in an 8/88-16-7 Epoch! This is when his fall noticeably began, a fall from which he would never recover. The self (1) was engaged in turmoil and chaos (7). Jackson's destiny, as related by his numbers, could not be more clear.

The downslide continued. On 20 November 2003, at age 45, Michael Jackson was arrested on child molestation charges by the Santa Barbara Police Department. On 13 June 2005, at age 46, a jury found Jackson not guilty on all charges. His trial had been a mega-happening with 2,200 reporters covering the event outside the courtroom (Wikipedia). Continuing a reputation of bizarre behavior, Jackson came to court late on occasion and at other times wearing pajama bottoms and a sport coat, walking with the help of body guards and lawyers and "looking more like a zombie from his *Thriller* video than the self-proclaimed King of Pop" (CBS, Vince Gonzales). "Death row inmates have moved to the execution chamber with more confidence than Michael Jackson moved to the defense table this morning" (CBS, Steve Corbett). Much of his demeanor seemed to be related to his medication and history with drug addiction.

Michael Jackson Mugshot: 20 November 2003, age 45

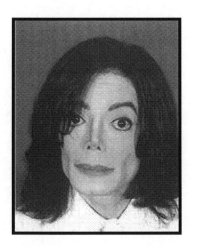

Michael Jackson's bizarre mugshot during his arrest on child molestation charges by the Santa Barbara Police Department.

Richard Andrew King

MASTER NUMBERS IN MICHAEL JACKSON'S CHART

Michael Jackson's numerology chart houses every master number. His Life Matrix houses a master number in every component. Most unusual are the two sets of double masters—the 66-3^2 Material Soul and the 44-8^2 Material Nature in his Basic Matrix.

All of this master number power served as both a blessing and a curse for Jackson. The positive side of each number made him a great talent, but the negative side of each number made him a tragic figure with a controversial and bizarre life (next page).

Master Numbers in Michael Jackson's Chart	
11	Nature 1st Epoch All four Challenge PEs
22	2nd Pinnacle 3rd Pinnacle PE 3rd Epoch PE
33	"Michael" Soul 4th Pinnacle PE
44	Material Nature 44-8^2
55	1st Epoch PE "King of Pop"
66	Material Soul 66-3^2
77	Performance/Experience (PE)
88	2nd Epoch PE 2nd Name "Joseph" PE
99	1st Pinnacle PE

Richard Andrew King

NUMBERS OF ARREST AND DEATH

It is not necessarily one number or number pattern that creates havoc in our lives but the simultaneous occurrence of a number or number pattern, i.e. *stacking*. On both the day Jackson's arrest warrant was announced, Wednesday, 19 November 2003, and his death on Thursday, 25 June 2009, Michael Jackson had a quintstack (five) of 7 energy, most of which housed a 16 root. The 16-7 number pattern is referred to in The King's Numerology[tm] system as the *Great Purifier* because it brings the fires of purification into our lives, fires which usually create testing, trials, turmoils, suffering and tears—all designed to cleanse us and balance our karmas. Marilyn Monroe and Princess Diana both had the 16-7 root in their Lifepaths. How many other famous icons featured in this work also had the 16-7 energy in their charts? Are you seeing the connection yet?

Michael Jackson
Announcement of Arrest Warrant
19 November 2003, Wednesday, age 45

1	Epoch Timeline PE (31 to 57)	8/16-7
2	Name Timeline PE - Joseph (34 to 61)	1/16-7
3	UTL Cycle Month PE (October)	8/16-7
4	PTL Universal Month (October)	16-7/6
5	Universal Day PE (19 November 2003)	8/16-7

Michael Jackson
Numbers at Death
25 June 2009, Thursday, age 50

1	Epoch Timeline PE (31 to 57)	8/88-16-7
2	Name Timeline PE - Joseph (34 to 61)	1/16-7
3	Letter Timeline – "P" (47 to 53)	16-7/11-2
4	Crown Pinnacle (age 49 on)	16-7/33-6
5	Day of Death – 25th of June	7/33-6

Michael Jackson: *Bad* **era jacket**

(Photo courtesy of Wikimedia Commons)

Michael at the White House – 1984

(Photo courtesy of Wikimedia Commons)

Richard Andrew King

SUMMARY

It is the way of the world—kingdoms and kings, cultures and queens, celebrities and civilizations, all rise and fall. Karmic Law cares not for princes or paupers, heroes or heroines, somebodies or nobodies, cheers or sneers. We all are bound by laws far greater than our vision or our egos can perceive . . . let alone control. When we inflate ourselves to levels equal to godlike status, we fall. It is impossible not to. Michael Jackson had huge talent, drive, magnetism and public appeal. However, like so many before him and just as many after him, he let it all get away from him. His life was not only a testament to art and accomplishment but also to the consequence of allowing his fame and fortune to run away with him and ultimately destroy him.

Jackson's life was a mirror and manifestation of a culture which has become saturated with personal indulgence, pleasure, a lack of discipline and self-control, good sense, abuses of medications and drugs; where emotion overpowers reason; where there is public obsession to adore and consume an individual without regards to the individual's rights of privacy and normalcy; where superficial celebrity supersedes substantive character and where fame is glorified over that which is divine. Could it not be argued that the public who worships human beings and assists in the expansion of their egos and ultimate decline, demise and death share in the responsibility of such tragedy? As a society, would it not be beneficial for us to reexamine how we perceive celebrities?

If Michael Joseph Jackson's life has any lasting and universal worth, let it be to awaken people to the reality that humanity must not be overshadowed by celebrity, that an individual's personal health and privacy, regardless of his station in life, must take precedence over public craving, and that human existence, as priceless and precious as it is, must never take a back seat to the fleeting facade of bright lights, fanatical fans and star-studded marquees.

The numbers and IR sets manifesting Jackson's rise to fame and fortune in his early life are the 1/99-9 in his first Pinnacle and the 11-2/55-1 in his first Epoch, corroborated by his 33 master numbers in his first name of *Michael*, as well as his Basic Matrix 33-6 Soul, his 66-3^2 dual Material Soul energies, his 11-2 IR set of inspiration and his 44-8^2 dual Material Nature IR sets.

Some of the interesting components in the numerology chart of Michael Jackson are . . .

- Jackson's chart contains every master number

- All of Jackson's Life Matrix components house a master number

- Jackson has dual Life Linkage Challenges: 3/2 and 6/5 (very rare)

- Jackson's enormous fame and fortune are clearly visible in his 1st Epoch (11-2/55-1) and 1st Pinnacle (1/99-9)

- The turmoil, decline and tragic fall of his life are seen in the PE tristack of his 2nd Epoch 8/88-7 Influence/Reality (IR) set, his Name Timeline 1/88-7 PE of *Joseph* and the 1/7 IR set of the "J" in "Joseph" (three 7s in a PE tristack portend trouble)

- Both the day Jackson's arrest warrant was announced and the date of his death house a quintstack of 7 energy in various components, most of which housed a 16 root (the Great Purifier)

MICHAEL JACKSON – QUOTES

I was a veteran before I was a teenager.

I just wish I could understand my father.

My mother's wonderful. To me she's perfection.

Just because it's in print doesn't mean it's the gospel.

I'm just like anyone. I cut and I bleed. And I embarrass easily.

And my goal in life is to give to the world what I was lucky to receive: the ecstasy of divine union through my music and my dance.

Richard Andrew King

The meaning of life is contained in every single expression of life. It is present in the infinity of forms and phenomena that exist in all of creation.

I've helped many, many, many children, thousands of children, cancer kids, leukemia kids.

Everyone who knows me will know the truth, which is that my children come first in my life and that I would never harm any child.

I will say again that I have never, and would never, harm a child. It sickens me that people have written untrue things about me.

I'm never pleased with anything. I'm a perfectionist. It's part of who I am.

The greatest education in the world is watching the masters at work.

You know, let's put it this way, if all the people in Hollywood who have had plastic surgery, if they went on vacation, there wouldn't be a person left in town.

Why can't you share your bed? The most loving thing to do is to share your bed with someone. It's very charming. It's very sweet. It's what the whole world should do.

I have always maintained my innocence and vehemently denied that these events ever took place. I reluctantly chose to settle the false claims only to end the terrible publicity and to continue with my life and career.

HISTORIC ICON #9

MUHAMMAD ALI

Born: Cassius Marcellus Clay, Jr. – 17 January 1942

Died – 3 June 2016, age 74

----

* The Greatest of All Time

* 3 Time World Heavyweight Boxing Champion

* Olympic Gold Medal – Rome, 1960

* Presidential Citizens Medal – 8 January 2005

* Presidential Medal of Freedom – 9 November 2005

* Otto Hahn Peace Medal in Gold (DGVN) – 17 December 2005

(Photo courtesy of Wikimedia Commons)

I'm the greatest, I'm a bad man, and I'm pretty.

Richard Andrew King

In the words of the 1960s legendary television hero, ex-cavalry scout Will Sonnett (played by Walter Brennan in *The Guns of Will Sonnett* series on ABC) . . . *No brag, just fact*. The four simple words of this truth apply to one of the greatest boxing champions of all time— Muhammad Ali who was, undoubtedly and unquestionably, the most loquacious boxing champion of all time. When Ali boisterously declared, *I'm the greatest*, he was simply stating old Will Sonnet's maxim, *No brag, just fact*.

Ali's life has been a statement of personal struggle, controversy, success, failure, dominance in his sport and challenges in his personal life. A flamboyant icon and skilled boxer, Ali's destiny has taken him through the gamut of public hero, to villain and back to hero. Always true to his beliefs, Muhammad Ali is one of the most unforgettable sports figures of all time.

PROVOCATIVE QUESTIONS

- What double Basic Matrix master number reveals Ali's uniqueness?
- From where does Ali's wordsmith personality originate?
- Where does Ali's warrior path come from?
- What number pattern illustrates Ali's controversial life?
- What do the numbers 2-6-8 reveal about Ali's professional boxing success and his personal relationships, especially his marriages?
- What IR set indicates a social disconnect and public controversy?
- What IR set illustrates Ali's reclusive life in his later years?
- What IR set reveals the public's love and admiration for Ali?

Muhammad Ali was born Cassius Marcellus Clay, Jr. on 17 January 1942 in Louisville, Kentucky. When Cassius was twenty-two years of age, he joined the Muslim faith and changed his name to Muhammad Ali, which means "Praiseworthy One." This was in March of 1964 after he defeated World Heavyweight Boxing Champion, Sonny Liston, on 25 February to become the World Heavyweight Boxing Champion.

Name changes can sometimes play a major role in one's life but they are rare. In an overwhelming number of cases, an individual's destiny is established from the full original name at birth and the birth date. Muhammad Ali's destiny, therefore, is derived from his original birth name, Cassius Marcellus Clay, Jr., which houses a Basic Matrix revealing a life of struggle, as well as a powerful, charismatic, introspective and original individual whose purpose in life was to play a major role in effecting change.

Basic Matrix: Cassius Marcellus Clay, Jr. (Muhammad Ali)

LP	Exp.	PE	Soul	MS	Nature	MN	Voids
7	3	55-1	3	55-1	9	7	2-6-8

The 55-1: PE and Material Soul

Distinctively clear in Ali's Basic Matrix is the master number 55-1, the energy representing an extremely unique and original individual. Ali's 55-1 is located in his PE, so we instantly know that the reality of his life and the performance he will give during his life's journey will be one of dramatic change and new direction. And how true is this! Ali grew up in a time when racial discrimination was extremely heavy, especially in the Southern region of the United States. His role as a world class champion certainly helped promote a more racially balanced perspective throughout the United States and the world.

What is also interesting regarding Ali's 55-1 is that he has a second set in his Material Soul, which means that not only was his role in life to be unique, different, original and trend-setting, but his most basic needs, drives and desires were exactly the same as his role in life. This gave him a strong purpose and direction. It's unusual that a person has matching master numbers in both the PE and the Material Soul, and the 55-1 is the most powerful energy for initiating change, action and new direction there is.

The 55-1 is also instrumental in Ali's enormous achievements within his life and profession. He started boxing at age twelve, won multiple Golden Glove awards and capped off his amateur career by winning an Olympic Gold Medal in 1960 in Rome, Italy, becoming the World Light Heavyweight Olympic Boxing Champion.

Richard Andrew King

Ali's professional boxing career was impressive. He was a three-time World Heavyweight Champion with a total of 61 fights, of which 56 were wins (37 knockouts, 19 decisions) and only 5 were losses (4 decisions, 1 TKO). He had zero draws. Furthermore, he boxed during a time which is considered by many to be the *Golden Age of Boxing*—Muhammad Ali sharing the spotlight with other notable fighters such as Joe Frazier, George Foreman, Kenny Norton, Larry Holmes, Floyd Patterson and Archie Moore among others.

The dangerous side of the 55-1, especially when stacked in a chart, is the possibility of a run-a-way ego—an unfortunate by-product of many of the iconic individuals featured in this work. Ali was certainly not immune to this flaw of the ego which plagues humanity as well. Following is just a sampling of Ali quotes revealing his opinion of himself.

I'm the greatest, I'm a bad man, and I'm pretty.

I am the greatest. I said that even before I knew I was.

It's hard to be humble, when you're as great as I am.

I'm not the greatest; I'm the double greatest. Not only do I knock 'em out, I pick the round.

I am the astronaut of boxing. Joe Louis and Dempsey were just jet pilots. I'm in a world of my own.

As an example of his post-fight jargon and narcissism, after defeating Sonny Liston on 25 February 1964 to become the World Heavyweight Champion at age 22, Ali effused . . .

> *I knew I had him in the first round. Almighty God was with me. I want everyone to bear witness, I am the greatest! I'm the greatest thing that ever lived. I don't have a mark on my face, and I upset Sonny Liston, and I just turned twenty-two years old. I must be the greatest. I showed the world. I talk to God everyday. I know the real God. I shook up the world, I'm the king of the world. You must listen to me. I am the greatest! I can't be beat!* [Wikipedia]

The 3: Expression and Soul

One of the most characteristic attributes of Muhammad Ali was his very talkative personality and wordsmithing as was illustrated in his post-fight exclamatory remarks with Joe Frazier. Ali was a poet of sorts and would often use language as a weapon in his war chest, giving him the unbecoming moniker, *The Louisville Lip*.

For example, regarding his third fight with Joe Frazier on 1 October 1975, billed as the *Fight of the Century* and called the *Thrilla in Manila*, Ali mused:

> *It will be a killa... and a chilla... and a thrilla...*
> *when I get the gorilla in Manila.*

This type of strategy was commonplace for Ali. He loved taking pot shots at his rivals, using his sharp tongue and wit as weapons to attack his opponents' minds and psyches brutally, brashly, rashly.

Of Sonny Liston he exclaimed:

> *Sonny Liston's so ugly that when he cries*
> *the tears run down the back of his head!*

Richard Andrew King

Of Joe Frazier he commented:

> *Joe Frazier's so ugly, they ought to donate his face to the World Wildlife Fund!*

Of George Foreman:

> *I've seen George Foreman shadow boxing, and the shadow won!*

Of Mike Tyson, Ali noted:

> *Mike Tyson is too ugly to become champion. He's got gold teeth. He's got bald spots all over his head. I used to call Joe Frazier "The Gorilla" but next to Tyson, Joe was a beautiful woman!*

Ali didn't restrict his words to opponents. Of Howard Cosell he stated:

> *Journalist Howard Cosell was gonna be a boxer when he was a kid, only they couldn't find a mouthpiece big enough!*
>
> (Brainyquote)

So where does all this incendiary language originate? Several places in Ali's chart accommodate such trash talking but certainly one of the major numbers is the 3—the energy of language, communication, narcissism, words, image. Ali has a 3 Soul and a 3 Expression so he loves to talk and communicate. But most people who have a 3 Soul and 3 Expression are not caustic like Ali was. One of the numbers supporting his "Louisville Lip" is the number 7.

The 7: Lifepath and Material Nature

As we've discussed, the 7 Lifepath is potentially the most difficult of the nine Lifepaths. Not only does it contain the energy of conflict and chaos, it is the number of the internalized warrior. It can be cold, cruel, calculating brutal and harsh. The 7 occupies Ali's Lifepath and his Material Nature (personality), again creating a double stack of intensity. He was in many ways a loner, which resonates with one who goes it alone, fights alone, is tested alone. Ali struggled in all aspects of his life. His opponents in the ring were simply another part of the puzzle of tumult that the 7 Lifepath can generate.

The 9 Nature

The 9 represents power. It dominates. Ali loved to dominate—not just with his mouth and gloves but with his movement and skill as well. For anyone who is going to be a dominant force in any field, the 9 is a welcomed partner, for it is almost impossible to dominate without it.

The 2-6-8 Voids

The 2-6-8 voided triumvirate played a key role in Ali's career and personal life, especially his four marriages. Muhammad Ali's birth name, *Cassius Marcellus Clay, Jr.,* has no B, K, or T (2); F, O or X (6) and no H, Q or Z (8). The 2, 6 and 8 are all social numbers.

2	Rules close personal relationships, especially concern for others and their welfare
6	Rules personal love, compassion, nurturing
8	Rules management, orchestration, connection

When voided, the 2 has no concern for the welfare of others; the 6 void doesn't care to nurture or have compassion; the 8 void reveals a disconnection with others. In a fighter's case, this can create an advantage because fighters cannot be concerned with their adversaries and Ali wasn't.

It's just a job. Grass grows, birds fly, waves pound the sand. I beat people up.

The 2, 6 and 8 voids were major players not only in Ali's professional boxing life but his personal life, especially in connection to the controversy over his refusal to be drafted into the United States military during the Vietnam war era. Ali publicly declared himself a conscientious objector. His reasoning was that his Muslim religion denied the killing of others. Yet, his own words voice a clear professional irony: *It's just a job. Grass grows, birds fly, waves pound the sand. I beat people up.* This begs the obvious question, "What's the difference between being a soldier and beating people up?"

Richard Andrew King

Too, many Americans have served in our armed forces because they felt it was their duty to support the country that graced them with the opportunity of being free to pursue their lives as they chose. Elvis Presley, Clark Gable, Jimmy Stewart, Humphrey Bogart, Henry Fonda, Paul Newman, Kirk Douglas, George C. Scott and Ronald Regan among others all served their country and were not only grateful but proud to do so.

Ali's refusal to serve his country infuriated many Americans. Ali was stripped of his Heavyweight Boxing Championship titles and arrested. His case was eventually dismissed by the United States Supreme Court, but his failure to serve created much hostility in his life for years and deprived him of furthering his boxing career while in his prime—from June of 1967 to June of 1971 between the ages of 25 to 29.

It was the 2, 6 and 8 voids that certainly played a role in Ali's troubles. There was a disconnect between himself and other Americans and it cost him. How much greater would Ali's legacy have been had he been able to fight during the lost years of legal battles over his refusal to serve? The 8 and 2 voids combine to form another major puzzle piece in Ali's life. For that, we must review his Life Matrix.

LIFE MATRIX
Voids: 2-6-8
CASSIUS MARCELLUS CLAY, JR.
17 JANUARY 1942

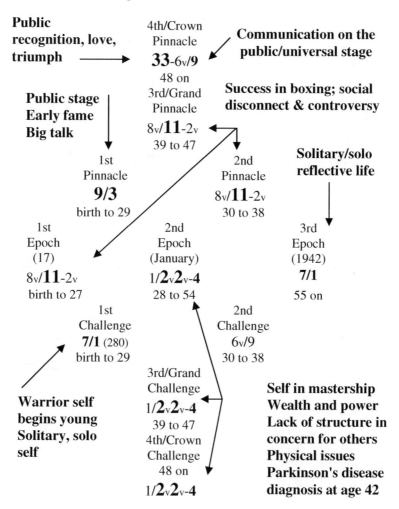

Public recognition, love, triumph →

4th/Crown Pinnacle
33-6v/**9**
48 on

Communication on the public/universal stage

3rd/Grand Pinnacle
8v/**11**-2v
39 to 47

Success in boxing; social disconnect & controversy

**Public stage
Early fame
Big talk**

1st Pinnacle
9/3
birth to 29

2nd Pinnacle
8v/**11**-2v
30 to 38

Solitary/solo reflective life

1st Epoch
(17)
8v/**11**-2v
birth to 27

2nd Epoch
(January)
1/**2**v**2**v-4
28 to 54

3rd Epoch
(1942)
7/1
55 on

1st Challenge
7/1 (280)
birth to 29

2nd Challenge
6v/**9**
30 to 38

**Warrior self begins young
Solitary, solo self**

3rd/Grand Challenge
1/**2**v**2**v-4
39 to 47
4th/Crown Challenge
48 on
1/**2**v**2**v-4

**Self in mastership
Wealth and power
Lack of structure in concern for others
Physical issues
Parkinson's disease diagnosis at age 42**

THE 8v/11-2v IR SET

On many levels, Muhammad Ali has been embroiled in controversy during his life. The 8v/11-2v IR set is the major player representing disconnection (8v) and division/separation/confrontation (2v). It helped him become successful as a fighter because his 55-1 energy of self and attainment propelled him forward, aided by a lack of concern for his opponents in the 8v/11-2v IR set. The number 2 is the energy of war and peace—the two sides of its energetic coin. A 2 void with its 11

Richard Andrew King

master root is highly intense and references one person vs. another person or one ideology vs. another ideology. Ali's life reflected both the personal and ideological aspects of the 11-2 through his fighting and draft-dodging efforts. This 8v/11-2v IR set is present in his 1st Epoch from birth to 27, in his 2nd and 3rd Pinnacles from age 30 to 47.

Fighting and ideology issues aside, Ali's marriages were also affected by the 2-6-8 voids. He simply had a difficult time understanding how close personal relationships worked (2), the love and nurturing involved within them (6) and their management (8). His fourth and final marriage with Yolanda Ali was in 1986 when Ali was 44. This was just three years before the end of the 8v/11-2v IR set that had been plaguing him since his birth, an IR set reflecting disconnection (8v) and separation (2v) that was center to his three failed marriages. How could his marriages have survived with such an 8v/2v energy field present in his life? Obviously, they could not.

MUHAMMAD ALI – NAME TIMELINE

Muhammad Ali's Name Timeline offers major clues to both his professional success and marital challenges. The first thing of note is the Name Timeline of the name *Cassius*. It reflects a 1/8v IR set which contains a double 44 master root. Powerful!

Name Timeline (NTL): Cassius Marcellus Clay, Jr.				
	First	Middle	Last	Suffix
Names	Cassius	Marcellus	Clay	Jr.
Timeline	birth to 19	20 to 51	52 to 65	66 to 75
General	19	32	14	10
IR Set	1	5	5	1
	8v	3	3	8v
Master PEs	44^2	6v6v		44
	Boxing success and Olympic Gold on 5 Sept. 1960	All of Ali's 3 divorces were in this period. The 6 void is the primary cause.		

The $1/44^2$-8v IR set shows the individual (1) in success (8) founded on extreme structure and discipline (44). Ali was a very hard-working athlete. His early boxing coach, Joe Martin, had this to say about Ali: *He was easily the hardest worker of any kid I ever taught.* Obviously, Ali's enduring success was founded on a strong work ethic. Did Ali enjoy his workouts? Here's his statement:

> *I hated every minute of training, but I said, "Don't quit.*
> *Suffer now and live the rest of your life as a champion."*

Ali's Name Timeline reveals the same 1/8v set via the "Jr." suffix which is active from age 66 to 75. At age 76, he will cycle back around to the 1/8v of his first birth name, Cassius, which would have been active for another 19 years through his 94th birthday. Ali died at age 74.

Ali's Name Timeline of *Marcellus* began at age 20 and lasted through age 51. It's IR set is a 5/66-3 Because of his 6 void, the IR set could also be written as 5/6v6v-3 (changes in love). This was the timeline of his three divorces.

PARKINSON'S DISEASE

Unfortunately, Muhammad Ali was diagnosed with Parkinson's Disease in 1984 at the age of 42, just three years after he entered his 1/22-4 Grand Challenge. Because of his 2 void, this IR set can be written as 1/2v2v-4. The number 4 rules the body and the 2 rules relationship, thus signifying relationship issues with his body. This was further complicated by a 4/7 IR set cycling through his Annual Cycle Patterns. The 4/7 shows distress in the body as the 4 must pass through his 3 Expression of health to generate a condition of stress, the 7.

Also contributing to his health issues is the 5/3 IR set in his Name Timeline and the 7/1 IR set in his 3rd Epoch. When all these numeric puzzle pieces are put together, they help describe his unfortunate disease status.

Richard Andrew King

LATER LIFE: PUBLIC RECOGNITION AND ACCLAIM

Muhammad Ali's destiny has been bitter-sweet. Fortunately for him, his Crown Pinnacle is a 6/9 in simple terms. This shows personal love (6) in the public realm of recognition and acclaim (9). Freely translated this makes him a beloved public figure.

Even more fortunate is that the 6 maintains a 33 master root. It is this energy of the 33-6v/9 that also is reflected in Ali's charity and humanitarian work, his public appearances, travels and many awards, among which are the *Presidential Citizens Medal* awarded to him on 8 January 2005 by President George W. Bush, the *Presidential Medal of Freedom* on 9 November 2005 awarded at the White House, and the *Otto Hahn Peace Medal in Gold*, awarded on 17 December 2005 by the UN Association of Germany in Berlin.

MASTER NUMBERS: CASSIUS MARCELLUS CLAY, Jr. (Muhammad Ali)

Following is a list of the master numbers in the King's Numerology[tm] chart of Cassius Marcellus Clay, Jr.

Master Numbers in Muhammad Ali's Chart	
11	1st Epoch PE 2nd Pinnacle PE 3rd (Grand) Pinnacle PE
22	2nd Epoch PE 3rd (Grand) Challenge PE 4th (Crown) Challenge PE
33	4th (Crown) Pinnacle
44	Double stack PE of "Cassius" PE of "Jr."
55	Life Performance/Experience (PE) Material Soul
66	PE of "Marcellus"
77	none
88	none
99	none

SUMMARY

Muhammad Ali has truly been an icon of his time and some people argue the best boxer of all time. His personal and professional life were very divisive and filled with criticism. His "Louisville Lip" and unbridled self-adulation were both magnetic and repulsive. Yet, Muhammad Ali's life has also been overflowing with inspiration. He is truly one-of-a-kind, just as his 55-1 IR set in his Material Soul and PE depict.

Richard Andrew King

Some of the interesting components in the numerology chart of Muhammad Ali are . . .

- The 55-1 dual presence in both his life PE and Material Soul
- The 8v/11-2v IR sets which played a major role in both his professional and personal life
- The 1/2v2v-4 Grand and Crown Challenges
- His 44^2 *Cassius* Name Timeline PE
- The 33-6v/9 Crown Pinnacle reflecting a later life of public love and acclaim
- His voids of 2, 6 and 8 which played major roles in the relationship aspect of his life

MUHAMMAD ALI – QUOTES

Float like a butterfly, sting like a bee.

I am the greatest. I said that even before I knew I was.

I figured that if I said it enough, I would convince the world that I really was the greatest.

I'm not the greatest; I'm the double greatest. Not only do I knock 'em out, I pick the round.

It's hard to be humble, when you're as great as I am.

A man who views the world the same at fifty as he did at twenty has wasted thirty years of his life.

Age is whatever you think it is. You are as old as you think you are.

Hating people because of their color is wrong. And it doesn't matter which color does the hating. It's just plain wrong.

He who is not courageous enough to take risks will accomplish nothing in life.

I am the astronaut of boxing. Joe Louis and Dempsey were just jet pilots. I'm in a world of my own.

I hated every minute of training, but I said, "Don't quit. Suffer now and live the rest of your life as a champion."

I never thought of losing, but now that it's happened, the only thing is to do it right. That's my obligation to all the people who believe in me. We all have to take defeats in life.

The fight is won or lost far away from witnesses – behind the lines, in the gym and out there on the road, long before I dance under those lights.

I'm so fast that last night I turned off the light switch in my hotel room and was in bed before the room was dark.

If you even dream of beating me you'd better wake up and apologize.

It isn't the mountains ahead to climb that wear you out; it's the pebble in your shoe.

It's just a job. Grass grows, birds fly, waves pound the sand. I beat people up.

It's not bragging if you can back it up.

It's lack of faith that makes people afraid of meeting challenges and I believed in myself.

Richard Andrew King

Service to others is the rent you pay for your room here on earth.

I know where I'm going and I know the truth and I don't have to be what you want me to be. I'm free to be what I want.

Wars of nations are fought to change maps. But wars of poverty are fought to map change.

(After defeating Sonny Liston for the first time: 25 February 1964) . . .

I knew I had him in the first round. Almighty God was with me. I want everyone to bear witness, I am the greatest! I'm the greatest thing that ever lived. I don't have a mark on my face, and I upset Sonny Liston, and I just turned twenty-two years old. I must be the greatest. I showed the world. I talk to God everyday. I know the real God. I shook up the world, I'm the king of the world. You must listen to me. I am the greatest! I can't be beat!

[Wikipedia]

We have one life; it soon will be past; what we do for God is all that will last.

HISTORIC ICON #10

O P R A H   W I N F R E Y

Born: Oprah Gail Winfrey – 29 January 1954

----

* Queen of Media

* Global Philanthropist

* Billionaire Entrepreneur

(Photo courtesy of Wikimedia Commons)

I always knew I was destined for greatness.

Think like a queen. A queen is not afraid to fail.
Failure is another steppingstone to greatness.

Richard Andrew King

For an individual to be known by a single name is powerful, indeed. Just think of the cavalcade of great souls in this category—names such as Einstein, Churchill, Newton, Diana, da Vinci, Earhart, Elvis, Sinatra, Liberace, Pelé, Cleopatra and now . . . Oprah. Certainly, the one-name moniker is indicative of an individual's recognition on the global historic stage.

Oprah Winfrey is a world icon, a brand, an institution. She needs no introduction; her influence, no discussion. She is a one-of-a-kind human being and her fame is both globally prodigious and renowned. But what of her success? Happenstance? Of course not. Hopefully, we know by now that nothing is coincidental in this universe. Numbers rule our destiny and Oprah's destiny was set long before she was born, and her enormous success and fame are distinctively revealed in her numbers, as they are in our other icons.

If there has ever been a queen of media, it is Oprah Winfrey. No woman in history has made more of an impact on so many lives through so many avenues of communication as she. The Oprah aura has exhibited itself through entrepreneurial enterprise, television, theater, film, music, radio and print media. Additionally, she has been heavily involved with education, philanthropy and humanitarian outreach. Her influence has lifted her to the throne of a multi-media empire and a billion dollar fortune. Unquestionably and irrefutably, Oprah Winfrey is one of the most celebrated women of her time and, arguably, in her day she was *the* most admired and beloved woman in America and perhaps the world (*The Age of the Female II: Heroines of the Shift*).

Born Oprah Gail Winfrey on 29 January 1954 on the family farm in Kosciusko, Mississippi, Oprah's destiny is filled with the energy of words, communication, relationship and entrepreneurial success.

PROVOCATIVE QUESTIONS

- What numbers reveal Oprah's extreme business success?

- What number pattern has driven her to be the best in media?

- Which IR sets are at the core of her life's journey?

- Which combination of numbers and IR sets reveal Oprah's difficulties and sexual abuse in her early life?

- What concentration of master numbers has been responsible for her achievement in the communication and media field?

- Which numbers in her Basic Matrix have driven her relationship with others, particularly women?

ENTREPRENEURIAL SUCCESS

One of the common aspects to people with a lifetime of success or attainment in any field of endeavor is *lifetime linkage*—the same numerical pattern existing from birth to death within their numerology chart. We have seen this already with other celebrated individuals in this work.

Lifetime linkage creates continuity—an unbroken stream of energy. When the energy stream is unbroken, it flows and flows and flows like a river with neither impediment nor stoppage. Another metaphor is that life linkage is a seed which begins to grow with the first breath of life out of the womb and continues to grow and grow and grow throughout the life, becoming a massive tree over time, such as a Coast Redwood (*Sequoia sempervirens*) which can grow to hundreds of feet in height.

Richard Andrew King

LIFE MATRIX
Voids: 2 & 4
OPRAH GAIL WINFREY
29 JANUARY 1954

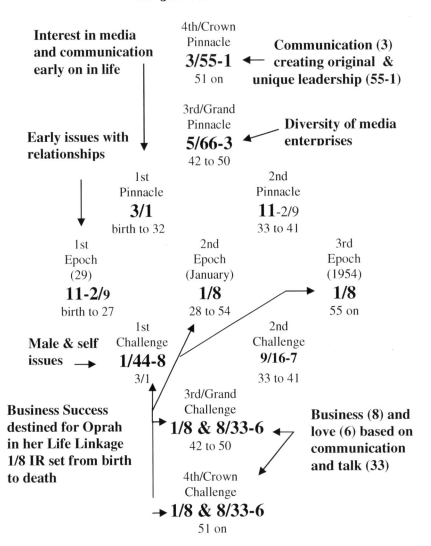

Interest in media and communication early on in life

4th/Crown
Pinnacle
3/55-1
51 on

Communication (3) creating original & unique leadership (55-1)

3rd/Grand
Pinnacle
5/66-3
42 to 50

Diversity of media enterprises

Early issues with relationships

1st
Pinnacle
3/1
birth to 32

2nd
Pinnacle
11-2/9
33 to 41

1st
Epoch
(29)
11-2/9
birth to 27

2nd
Epoch
(January)
1/8
28 to 54

3rd
Epoch
(1954)
1/8
55 on

Male & self issues →

1st
Challenge
1/44-8
3/1

2nd
Challenge
9/16-7
33 to 41

Business Success destined for Oprah in her Life Linkage 1/8 IR set from birth to death

3rd/Grand
Challenge
1/8 & 8/33-6
42 to 50

Business (8) and love (6) based on communication and talk (33)

4th/Crown
Challenge
1/8 & 8/33-6
51 on

3/55-1 CROWN PINNACLE: MEDIA ACHIEVEMENT

The first thing of note, which we've also seen before in the chart of Howard Hughes, is the 3/55-1 Crown Pinnacle IR set. Hughes was a media icon of his time. Remember his statement . . .

I intend to be the greatest golfer in the world,
the finest film producer in Hollywood,
the greatest pilot in the world,
and the richest man in the world.

Numbers are not arbitrary and it is no coincidence that Oprah Winfrey, who also maintains a 3/55-1 in her Crown Pinnacle, has become the greatest at what she does. The 3 rules image, communication, media; the 55-1 is a powerful statement of individuality. Of course there are major differences in the charts of Hughes and Winfrey, but their lives and destinies have clearly been representative of media success, independence and leadership.

1/8 LIFETIME LINKAGE: ENTREPRENEURIAL SUCCESS

It is the 1/8 IR set that is primarily responsible for Oprah's success. It represents the individual, the self, the initiator (1) actively involved in commercial enterprise and worldly success (8).
Oprah's 1/8 IR set is located in her . . .

- 1st Challenge
- 3rd (Grand) Challenge
- 4th (Crown) Challenge
- 2nd (Core) Epoch
- 3rd (Crown) Epoch

This 1/8 IR set therefore creates a quintstack of individual success for Oprah Winfrey and would for anyone whose chart also exhibited the same set of numbers. Lifetime linkage can sometimes be seen in a quadstack in one's Challenges, for example in the chart of Michael Jackson, but to have an IR set placed from birth to death in five of the eleven components of a Life Matrix is

Richard Andrew King

extraordinary. Basically, the destiny of Oprah Gail Winfrey was for her to be enormously successful and the 1/8 IR set is the primary energetic mover.

OPRAH'S GRAND PINNACLE/CHALLENGE (PC) COUPLET

The Grand PC Couplet (Grand Pinnacle and Grand Challenge) is the core of a person's energy world. Oprah's Grand Pinnacle of 5/66-3 and her sibling dual Grand Challenges of 1/8 and 8/33-6 are major power players in a numeric environment already based in power—the 22-4 Lifepath. At the core of her 22-4 Lifepath of work, service, power and wealth is the 5/66-3 Grand Pinnacle IR set referencing diversity and versatility (5) playing itself out in the realm of what else, media—the 3 with a 66 master root of personal love, nurturing, compassion. The Grand Pinnacle's sibling, the Grand Challenge, houses a double power business set comprised of the 1/8 and the 8/33-6. How could anyone not be successful with such numbers?

OPRAH'S BASIC MATRIX

Basic Matrix: Oprah Gail Winfrey

LP	Exp.	PE	Soul	MS	Nature	MN	Voids
22-4	7	11-2	11-2	33-6	5	9	2 & 4

22-4 Lifepath

No Lifepath expresses power and wealth more than the 22-4. It is *the* material powerhouse of the master numbers. It builds (4) on the foundation of relationship (2 and 2). It is a lifepath, a life script, an energy world of work, service, security, duty, constancy, effort and staying power.

7 Expression

Analytical, deep, reflective, thoughtful, intuitive, spiritual, calculating, prone to quiescent behavior, quiet moments of the self, a potential for being cold, callous, critical, inconsiderate and indifferent, sometimes cruel and ruthless if taken to the extreme are manifestations of the 7 Expression in both its positive and negative aspects—the simple numerical equivalent of Oprah Winfrey, which is also shared by 1/9th of the world's population (world population divided by 9, the number of single ciphers).

Sevens are thinkers. A perfect example of the 7 in manifestation is Auguste Rodin's famous statute, *The Thinker*. So many astute and successful souls have 7 in their chart. It gives them depth, sensitivity and an ability to think things through. This is why the 1/8 IR set is powerful. The 1 mixes with the 7 to create the 8. Therefore, the 1/8 IR set can also be depicted as 1/(7)/8, in which the 7 is the filter or funnel for the energy of action and independence (1) passing through it (the 7) to create an energy of orchestration, flow, administration and execution (8).

11-2: PE and Soul

The 2 rules relationship, others and female (yin) energy. For Oprah Winfrey, the 2 rules her desires, needs and wants (Soul) as well as the performance she would give on the great life stage (PE). When the Soul and PE are the same in a chart, it means the individual is comfortable with his/her life in a major way because the person's basic needs equate to the performance he or she will realize in life.

For Oprah, her life is centered in relationship, others and female energy. She is a perfect fit for this current age and millennium which is centered in the energy of the 2 whose numerical meanings are fully discussed in *The Age of the Female: A Thousand Years of Yin*, as well as KBN11. The Oprah Winfrey Show was itself centered in female energy and relationship. This is simply a reflection of Oprah's Soul and life PE—her primal desires and life reality respectively.

33-6 Material Soul

The moniker *Queen of Media* is further enhanced by Oprah's 33-6 Material Soul—an energy of love, compassion, nurturing, responsibility and care for others with a root of 33—the master number of communication and self-expression. Therefore, added to Oprah's desire for relationship, as revealed by her 2 Soul, is a second desire to love and nurture others and to be, in many cases, a mother and partner to all, especially children.

Richard Andrew King

<u>5 Nature; 9 Material Nature</u>

No two numbers in concert resonate with the masses more than the numbers 5 and 9. The 5 is the fulcrum of the *Alpha Numeric Spectrum* (basic numbers 1 to 9). It is called the *Number of Man*. It can move with equal ease up and down the numeric spectrum, touching all as it moves.

The number 9 is the *Grand Elemental*, the *Number of Mankind*. All numbers are contained within it and it reflects all numbers to themselves. It is the ruler of the numeric spectrum. Its symbols are the scepter, crown, throne and microphone. It is universal power.

Because Oprah Winfrey has the 5 and 9 in her Nature components, she is intrinsically in tune and in touch with the masses. She loves variety and reflects a dominant personality. Princess Diana also had the 5 and 9 dominant in her chart, as we shall see in her chapter. (Note: the life and destiny of Diana are fully explained in *The King's Book of Numerology, Volume 9: Numeric Biography, Princess Diana*, aka KBN9).

NAME TIMELINE: OPRAH GAIL WINFREY

The complete Name Timeline of Oprah Winfrey offers further clues as to her immense success. Notice in her NTL chart that every one of her names maintains a master number in its PE position.

Name Timeline (NTL): Oprah Gail Winfrey			
	First	Middle	Last
Names	Oprah	Gail	Winfrey
Timeline	Birth to 31	32 to 51	52 to 97
General	31	20	46
IR Set	4v	2v	1
	8	6	77-5
Master PEs	**44**	**33**	**77**
	4v4v		

The first master number of 44-8 is the PE of *Oprah*. Its influencing energy is the 4, creating a 4v/4v4v-8 IR set from her birth to age 31. The 44 is a powerful energy of work and success, which Oprah demonstrated after her initial years of domestic and personal problems.

The second master number is the 33 in the 2v/33-6 IR set of *Gail*. Once again, we have more evidence of the powerful communicative energy in her chart. Everywhere we look in Oprah's chart, the 33 is present—Name Timeline, Basic Matrix and Life Matrix. This 2v/33-6 IR set was active from ages 32 to 51, smack dab in the middle of her professional career.

The third master number PE is the 77 which exists in the 1/77-5 IR set in the name of *Winfrey*. It began at age 52 and will be active through Oprah's 97th year. This will be a time in which she will be inwardly active, especially mentally and spiritually. There will be new beginnings and changes for her, deep changes which could revolutionize her life on an inward basis, not so much an external one.

In this 1/5 IR set the 5 represents freedom and detachment and the 1 references the self. These are both independent numbers, not social numbers. They are also filled with the fire of action. Hence, one layer of Oprah's life from 52 on will reflect conditions unlike those in her earlier life. She will be more independent and free. Still, she will be involved in the world of business and commerce because both her 3rd (Crown) Epoch and 4th (Crown) Challenge are a 1/8—the IR set of entrepreneurial activity.

The manifestation of this 1/5 IR set is clearly indicated in her numbers and timelines. The series finale of her extremely successful and award-winning television hit, *The Oprah Winfrey Show*, aired on 25 May 2011 when Oprah was 57 years old. Her new venture, *The Oprah Winfrey Network* (aka OWN), began in January of 2011 (Wikipedia).

This 1/5 Name Timeline of *Winfrey* is created when the 1 of *Winfrey* passes through her 4 Lifepath of work and service creating the 5 of change, freedom and variety. Thus, she will still be working but in an environment that is more diverse and free.

Richard Andrew King

EARLY LIFE DIFFICULTIES

Oprah has been extremely open regarding her early years in which she lived in rural poverty with her grandmother, Hattie Mae Lee, having been the result of a brief sexual encounter between her biological mother and father. At age 6 she moved to Milwaukee, Wisconsin, and lived in an inner-city neighborhood with her mother, Vernita Lee. Oprah stated she was molested by her cousin, her uncle and a family friend beginning when she was nine years old (Wikipedia). This period of time was in her Letter Timeline (LTL) of the "P" in *Oprah* from age 7 to age 13, creating a 16-7/11-2v IR set. This is the same IR set that reflected problems for Marilyn Monroe. The difference was that Marilyn's IR set was a 7v/11-2 rather than Oprah's 7/11-2v—same pattern, different voids, but still problematic.

Creating more problems for Oprah in her early years was that her LTL of a 7/11-2v was corroborated by a 1st Epoch of 11-2v/9. This reveals the problems and tensions with others, particularly women and relationships, as they're ruled by the number 2. Traveling is indicated by the number 9. Oprah's day of birth is the 29th of January. The number 29 is an 11 in reduction housing a 7 subcap (created by subtracting the 2 from the 9). This created more problems for her. The 29 binary carries more tension in relationships than any other binary number. It exudes power (9) in relationship (2) with a clash of egos and ideologies (11).

Compounding the problematic energies of the 7/11-2v LTL of the letter "P" and the 2v/9 1st Epoch IR set was her 1/8 Challenge in which the 8 carried a 44 master root. With the number 4 being void in her chart, this created issues with her security and lack of discipline and self-control (4v4v-8).

When a 1 occurs in the 1st Challenge position, it often references male energy, which is problematic and not generally beneficial. This would account for the sexual abuse she experienced from her cousin, uncle and a family friend. Women particularly who have their 1st Challenge occupied by a 1 cipher will have some type of issue(s) with males, whether it is the father, brother, uncle, grandfather, step-father, boss or female with dominant 1 energy in her chart. It's not uncommon to see women with a 1 in the 1st Challenge position of their young lives having issues with males, authority figures or being a tomboy.

It must be remembered, however, that the 1 also represents the self, the star, the doer, the one who takes charge, who leads and inspires. Oprah Winfrey has certainly fit that role perfectly.

(Photo courtesy of Wikimedia Commons)

MASTER NUMBERS: OPRAH WINFREY

Oprah has every master number in some component of her King's Numerology^{tm} chart except for the master numbers 88 and 99.

Richard Andrew King

Master Numbers in Oprah Winfrey's Chart	
11	Soul Life Performance/Experience (PE) 2nd Pinnacle Transition root-1st Epoch-day of birth (29th) LTL PEs of the letters P, G and Y in her natal name
22	Lifepath
33	Material Soul NTL PE of *Gail* Grand Challenge PE Crown Challenge PE
44	NTL PE of *Oprah* 1st Challenge PE
55	Crown Pinnacle PE
66	Grand Pinnacle PE
77	NTL PE of *Winfrey*
88	none
99	none

SUMMARY

There is absolutely no doubt Oprah Gail Winfrey will go down in history as one of the greatest females of the latter 20th Century and early 21st Century. She has built a media empire of enormous size and touched countless numbers of individuals in the course of her destiny, which has bequeathed upon her a role to play on the great life stage focusing on the Yin, on females, others, relationships, support, caring, togetherness, partnership and cooperation.

(Photo courtesy of Wikimedia Commons)

Some of the interesting components in the numerology chart of Oprah Winfrey are . . .

- The 1/8 Lifetime Linkage in five Life Matrix components
- Her 3/55-1 Crown Pinnacle PE of communication and originality
- Her 5/66-3 Grand Pinnacle illustrating love of communication
- The 8/33-6 Grand and Crown Challenges showing a love of communication and interaction
- The master numbers 44, 33 and 77 in her Name Timeline PEs

Richard Andrew King

OPRAH WINFREY – QUOTES

I always knew I was destined for greatness.

Where there is no struggle, there is no strength.

We can't become what we need to be by remaining what we are.

Follow your instincts. That's where true wisdom manifests itself.

Surround yourself with only people who are going to lift you higher.

Real integrity is doing the right thing, knowing that nobody's going to know whether you did it or not.

Think like a queen. A queen is not afraid to fail. Failure is another steppingstone to greatness.

Excellence is the best deterrent to racism or sexism.

My philosophy is that not only are you responsible for your life, but doing the best at this moment puts you in the best place for the next moment.

Turn your wounds into wisdom.

The more you praise and celebrate your life, the more there is in life to celebrate.

I am a woman in process. I'm just trying like everybody else. I try to take every conflict, every experience and learn from it. Life is never dull.

I do not believe in failure. It is not failure if you enjoyed the process.

If you come to fame not understanding who you are, it will define who you are.

You are what you are by what you believe!

Lots of people want to ride with you in the limo, but what you want is someone who will take the bus with you when the limo breaks down.

It isn't until you come to a spiritual understanding of who you are – not necessarily a religious feeling, but deep down, the spirit within – that you can begin to take control.

Richard Andrew King

HISTORIC ICON #11

PRINCESS DIANA

Born: Diana Frances Spencer – 1 July 1961

Died: 31 August 1997, age 36

----

* Diana, Princess of Wales

* England's Rose - Queen of Hearts - People's Princess

(Photo courtesy of Wikimedia Commons)

Being a princess isn't all it's cracked up to be.

Richard Andrew King

Princess Diana was born Diana Frances Spencer on 1 July 1961. She died tragically in a car crash on 31 August 1997 at the tender age of thirty-six. Her death sent shock waves around the globe. Diana was heralded throughout the United Kingdom and the world as the *Queen of Hearts*, the *Princess of Love*, the *People's Princess* and *England's Rose*. She had a special quality of love and compassion that endeared her to millions of people. She also had a divine destiny that far exceeded the ordinary scope of her extraordinary life.

During her life, Princess Diana was often regarded as the most famous and most photographed woman in the world. The span and spell of her embrace were almost beyond comprehension, as was the profound importance of her life as a millennia bridge. It is estimated that millions of people worldwide watched her funeral. What person in the history of mankind has had such an audience in the aftermath of his or her death? Such a degree of adoring adulation is unquestionably, even profoundly, remarkable.

One of the interesting things about Diana's life is that of all the icons featured in this work, she was the least accomplished. She wasn't a renowned scientist, Camelot president, rock star, industrial tycoon, media magnet, famous aviator, vaunted military hero, champion athlete, sex siren, or political powerhouse. Diana was a common person. However, she had such a prodigious personality she was able to accomplish what no other individuals in the history of the British Empire had accomplished in their deaths—not Churchill, Shakespeare, Newton, Nelson, Tennyson, Johnson, etc.—cause the Union Jack (flag of Great Britain) to be lowered to half staff in honor of her life after she died.

Diana lived a fairytale dream turned nightmare. It's a common fantasy of young girls to marry a prince and live happily ever after. She did marry a prince in one of the most lavish weddings in history. Sadly, she ended up trading her fairytale life for a tarnished crown, faithless ring, broken dream, broken heart and a legacy of her son's lives she would never know. She died tragically in a high speed car chase in a Paris tunnel on 31 August 1997 at the age of 36, leaving many to wonder if her death were actually accidental.

Diana was not born into royalty. She was an aristocratic girl with common attributes who married into it. She expressed her feelings openly and unashamedly to the people she and the monarchy served while she was a princess. She touched people, she made them feel they were together in one family. She cared. She was sensitive and receptive to people's needs, feelings and desires. She was in touch with England's citizens in a way other members of the royal family were not. Basically, she was a normal human being with humanitarian sensibilities. Her tragic death was, therefore, a devastation for Great Britain. It is hoped that her legacy of love will be carried on by her sons William and Harry.

PROVOCATIVE QUESTIONS

- What Lifepath number revealed Diana's life of tragedy and tears?
- Why was Diana so loved, yet hounded by the press?
- What numbers reveal her childhood heartaches?
- What IR set is principally responsible for Diana's troubles?
- What's the connection between Diana and Marilyn Monroe?
- What is significant about the years Diana married and died?

PRINCESS DIANA: BASIC MATRIX

Basic Matrix: Diana Frances Spencer

LP	Exp.	PE	Soul	MS	Nature	MN	Voids
7	4	11-2	9	7	22-4	11-2	2 & 8

Richard Andrew King

Diana's 7 Lifepath: A Path of Tears

> *She lived in a lonely world, starved of love, possessing a need for company. In the privacy of her rooms she cried her eyes out, despairing that she would never be able to live her life without crisis* (*Diana, Her New Life*: Andrew Morton).

As life is destined to the breath, so the die of life is cast before our birth. In a universe strictly bound by the karmic law of sowing and reaping, cause and effect, there can be no innocent victims in this creation. As difficult as it may be to accept, the truth is we are all the makers of our destiny, the creators of the lives we lead. We are the architects of our fate and of this there is no mistake. The life of Princess Diana, as sad, tragic and remarkable as it was, was forged before she was born. Like General George Patton, she did believe in reincarnation, so on some level she had to know her life was a manifestation of past life experiences.

The sad and painful truth of Diana Frances Spencer's life was that it was destined to be a path of tears. Given the vibrations of her 7 Lifepath and its inner construct, there is absolutely no way she could have ever lived happily ever after, at least in this life.

Diana's impact and influence upon the Royal family, the British Monarchy, the British way of life and the world in general cannot be underestimated. After all, here was a young girl without a higher education who waged a war, single-handedly, against an entire Royal family and a thousand years of English tradition . . . and won. Impressive. No person in the history of the world has received more attention and adulation in their life and death than Diana, Princess of Wales. She was, indeed, loved by many. But why? Why was her life so tragic? Why was it, a path of tears?

Princess Diana's Lifepath was a 7, maintaining roots of 16 and 25. It is this 16-25-7 Lifepath which was arguably the main reason for her unhappy life. It is why she was described as: *a woman scorned but also a woman forlorn; a woman who had everything but happiness;* a woman who her friends saw as *slowly dying inside* and a woman who, of her own life, asked, *When will I get out of this hellhole?* (Chapter Five, "A Path of Tears" – *The King's Book of Numerology, Volume 9: Numeric Biography, Princess Diana*).

The King's Book of Numerology, Volume 10: Historic Icons – Part 1

7 Material Soul

Diana's Material Soul was a 7. This resonated with her 7 Lifepath. It is one of the main reasons she was sensitive, intuitive and comfortable with the metaphysical world. Diana had depth. She was not superficial. No 7 Soul person is superficial. They are often shy, retiring, sensitive, intuitive, solitary, private, deep, misunderstood and spiritually attuned. The thing 7 Soul people are not is superficial. Yet, in a superficial world this can cause problems because there can be stress caused by a tug-o-war between the outer world of material phenomena and the inner world of reflection and the spirit.

9 Soul

The number 9 represents universality—that which is common to everyone regardless of external veneers such as language, race, creed, color, gender. Therefore, a 9 Soul person will seek the public stage to some degree because their innermost desires harmonize with the masses as the number 9 is all numbers and therefore all people. Ambition, rulership and power can also be manifestations of the 9 Soul. In effect, Diana was ambitious and identified with the public spotlight.

9 and 22-4

The 22-4 rules power and wealth; the 4 rules structure, security, roots, order, stability and duty. Diana had a 22-4 Nature and a 4 Expression. She also had a 22-4 in her Grand Challenge influence and a 22-4 in her Crown Pinnacle PE. Interestingly, her Crown Pinnacle was a 9, thus creating a 9/22-4 Crown Pinnacle IR set of rulership, power, wealth and fame—the very ingredients of her life's path. The 22-4 in both a Crown Pinnacle and Grand Challenge position reveal that she was always in a state of tension between the positive and negative aspects of wealth and power. The master number 22-4 can create great wealth but it can also create great limitation. What princess has both anonymity and true freedom? Hence, the struggle.

11-2v PE and 11-2v Material Nature

There is a large amount of inspiration, achievement, intensity and emotion in the 11-2 energy. There is also the potential of stress and conflict. Diana had a 2 void in her chart and this would account for her emotional stress and instability from time to time. On the positive side, the 11-2

Richard Andrew King

gave Diana the wonderful sense of caring she had for others, a quality not generally associated with royalty, which is one reason she was so popular with the masses.

LIFE MATRIX
Voids: 2 & 8
DIANA FRANCES SPENCER
1 JULY 1961

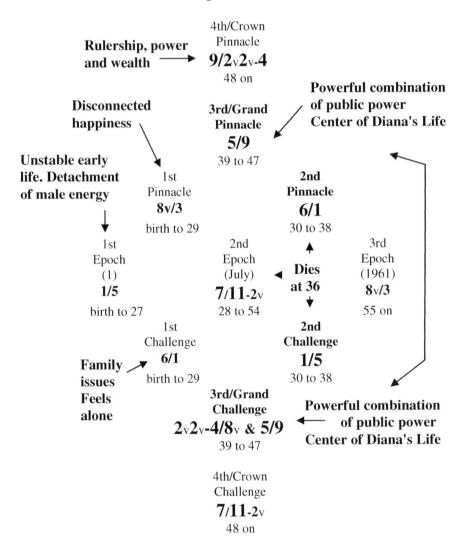

Rulership, power and wealth →

4th/Crown Pinnacle
9/2v2v-4
48 on

Powerful combination of public power Center of Diana's Life

Disconnected happiness

3rd/Grand Pinnacle
5/9
39 to 47

Unstable early life. Detachment of male energy

1st Pinnacle
8v/3
birth to 29

2nd Pinnacle
6/1
30 to 38

1st Epoch (1)
1/5
birth to 27

2nd Epoch (July)
7/11-2v
28 to 54

Dies at 36

3rd Epoch (1961)
8v/3
55 on

1st Challenge
6/1
birth to 29

2nd Challenge
1/5
30 to 38

Family issues Feels alone

3rd/Grand Challenge
2v2v-4/8v & 5/9
39 to 47

Powerful combination of public power Center of Diana's Life

4th/Crown Challenge
7/11-2v
48 on

THE DOUBLE-EDGED SWORD OF FAME: THE 5/9 GRAND PC COUPLET

Diana was both loved and hounded by the press and the relentless, often cruel and insensitive predatory conduct of the paparazzi. Why? This is very clear. Look at her Life Matrix Grand Pinnacle and Grand Challenge—the core energies of her 7 Lifepath. Notice they both house the 5/9 IR set. This is extremely rare and telling.

No two numbers identify the public more than the 5 and 9, which can be present separately in a chart in its various components. For example, Oprah Winfrey has a 5 Nature and a 9 Material Nature.

However, when the 5 and 9 are combined in the 5/9 IR set they reveal an energy that is intrinsically saturated and intertwined with people and the public stage—5 is the *Number of Man*; 9 is the *Number of Mankind*.

This 5/9 IR set is common to all people with a 4 Expression to some degree, but it may not show up in the Life Matrix, which is the framework of the Lifepath itself. It can also show up in any one of the eleven components of the Life Matrix, but when it occupies a Grand Pinnacle or Grand Challenge position it is very powerful because they represent the very center of the life script in both its positive and negative aspects. To have this 5/9 IR present in *both* components of the Grand PC Couplet simultaneously is very rare, indicating that the individual will be both positively and negatively affected by the public in a grand way. Diana was loved by the masses but hounded by the press and all of its relentlessly salivating gossip mongering.

Furthermore, this 5/9 Grand PC Couplet is the center of Princess Diana's 7 Lifepath—the most spiritually challenging Lifepath there is. Therefore, from a destiny standpoint it is clear that the public at large would be powerfully instrumental in her life. There was no way she could have avoided the fame thrust upon her—and this all could have been known from the moment of her birth once her chart was constructed.

Of major note is that Marilyn Monroe also had a 5/9 IR set in her chart except hers was located in her 1st Challenge, the period of her early life from birth through age 29. She was also the recipient

Richard Andrew King

of the same kind of public intensity and notoriety as Diana. In fact, Diana and Marilyn had very similar lives, destinies and numbers. More on this in a bit.

DOUBLE 55-1: NAME TIMELINE OF *FRANCES*

As we have seen in the charts of the extremely original individuals featured in this work, the 55-1 energy is common to all in their birth name except Marilyn Monroe. As aforementioned, however, Monroe does have a 55-1 in the Material Nature of her common/stage name.

Name Timeline (NTL): Princess Diana			
	First	Middle	Last
Names	Diana	Frances	Spencer
Timeline	birth to 20	21 to 50	51 to 85
General	20	30	35
IR Set	2	3	8
	9	$55\text{-}1^2$	$33\text{-}6^2$
Master #s	n/a	55	33
		Dies here	

Princess Diana not only has a 55-1 in her Name Timeline of *Frances*, but it is a double 55-1 indicated by the $55\text{-}1^2$ configuration. There is no question Diana was a true original and created massive change in the way the British Empire conducted its business. Princess Diana literally revolutionized the British Monarchy. Not only was the Union Jack lowered to half mast in respect of her life when she died, but the Queen of England (Elizabeth II) even bowed her head in respect as Diana's casket passed the Queen in her funeral procession—something a Queen never does. Yet, to her credit, the conduct of Queen Elizabeth was befitting a queen. To not have paid respects to Diana, who had captured the hearts and minds of the British people, would have been most unseemly, inappropriate and anything but queenly.

DOUBLE 33-6: NAME TIMELINE OF *SPENCER*

Augmenting Diana's double 55-1 in the NTL of *Frances* is her double 33-6 in her Name Timeline of *Spencer*. This can be written as $33\text{-}6^2$. This gave Diana a sense of great love and compassion on a personal level, as is seen in her following quotes.

Hugs can do great amounts of good - especially for children.

I knew what my job was; it was to go out and meet the people and love them.

Anywhere I see suffering, that is where I want to be, doing what I can.

The biggest disease this day and age is that of people feeling unloved.

7/11-2v: 2nd EPOCH AND CROWN CHALLENGE

The 7/11-2 IR set is a problematic energy reflecting stress, concern or even chaos in the realm of relationship to some degree or another. Marilyn Monroe had a 7v/11-2 IR set in her 1st Pinnacle and Grand Challenge. Michael Jackson had a 7/11-2 in the "P" Letter Timeline of *Joseph* when he died. Oprah Winfrey has a 7/11-2v in the "P" Letter Timeline of *Oprah*, which was during her troubled early life. Princess Diana had the 7/11-2v IR set in her 2nd Epoch and Crown Challenge. Every one of these individuals experienced extreme difficulties, sorrow, suffering, heartache and heartbreak during this 7/11-2 IR set and its variations.

The lives of Monroe, Jackson, Oprah and Diana are exceedingly well known. It was during some type of the 7/11-2 IR set that they all experienced problems with relationships. This is just one example illustrating the numeric reality of life and destiny and should be ample reason for those with inquiring, investigative and studious minds to expand their knowledge through numbers.

It is no secret that Princess Diana was plagued with personal problems throughout her life. The ugly divorce of her parents when she was very young, her marriage to Charles, relationship with the Royal Family, the relentless pursuit of the paparazzi, public betrayals and her secret romantic relationships were all a manifestation, in large part, due to the energy of the 7/11-2v IR set in her chart, i.e., the blueprint of her destiny.

Richard Andrew King

PROBLEMBATIC EARLY LIFE

Diana's early life set the sorrowful tone for the rest of her life. Her parents, having had two daughters already, were hoping for a boy on the third pregnancy and were disappointed when they had a girl, Diana. In her book, *Diana in Private*, Lady Colin Campbell relates:

> *Diana was a disappointment. Her parents, Viscount and Viscountess Althorp, had hoped for a son and heir to replace the boy, John, who had died the day he was born, eighteen months before on 12 January 1960. Instead, they got yet another girl.*

This was a significant event in Diana life's because she would look back and not feel loved. As Diana would always lament, *I was the girl who was supposed to be a boy*. As a result of this event, she always felt she was a nuisance, accepting a corresponding load of guilt and failure for disappointing her parents and family (*Diana, Her True Story*, Andrew Morton).

Compounding her suffering, when Diana was six years old, her mother had an affair and left home. An acrimonious and bitter divorce ensued. It was a difficult and emotionally stressful time for the young Diana, a memory that would never leave her. As she states . . .

> *My parents were busy sorting themselves out. I remember my mother crying. Daddy never spoke to us about it. We could never ask questions. Too many nannies. The whole thing was very unstable.* (Morton)

Diana's Name Timeline reflects the problems with her parents divorce in its 2/9 IR set of her first name, *Diana*. Because she has a 2 void, this 2/9 can be written as 2v/9, indicating that relationships and emotions (2) will express themselves through the 9 of endings, travel, family. As the last line of the previous quote states: *It was a childhood where she wanted nothing materially but everything emotionally*. Emotions are ruled by the number 2, and when the 2 is void emotional issues are very likely to become apparent. In fact, a very common condition for those who have voids is to crave or long for the qualities the void or voids represent. A person with a 6 void will often long for love and romance; a person with a 4 void for security, safety and stability; a person with a 3 void may wish for health, joy, happiness, children.

Diana's Life Matrix also reveals other explanations regarding the problems in her early life. These are seen in her 1/5 1st Epoch which references the instability Diana was feeling over her parent's divorce. Her own words validate this: *The whole thing was very unstable.* The 5 is the energy indicating the instability. It is the number of motion, movement, uncertainty. The 1 references her sense of self and identity.

Diana's 1st Challenge is a 6/1. Here again we see an emphasis on her, the 1, which springs from the 6 of home, heart, love, nurturing, emotion, the domestic environment and so forth. The number 1 also references male energy, and it was her father who received custody of the children in the divorce. Too, because the number 1 references male energy, it also indicates her brother and the love challenges and heartache he experienced, as shown by the 6/1 IR set.

The 8v/3 in Diana's 1st Pinnacle reveals a disconnect (8v) in her joy, happiness, well-being and health (3). The number 3 also rules children, and all of her siblings were negatively affected in some way by her parent's divorce.

Another indication of Diana's early life troubles and sorrows is that the divorce occurred in the "I" of *Diana*, creating a 9/7 IR set of turmoil, heartbreak, heartache, betrayal, potential adultery and general suffering. How often in the lives of the featured individuals in this work have we seen the number 7 associated with turmoil, stress, betrayal and sorrow? The 9/7 IR set can manifest as spiritual growth and expansion but that usually occurs through the testing energies of the 7 energy.

When all these numeric puzzle pieces are considered as a whole, it's clear that Diana's early life would be quite hard and have an impact on her later life. The 1st Epoch, Pinnacle and Challenge triad can be considered the trunk of the emerging tree of an individual's life, and when the trunk—the foundation of the tree, the life—is comprised of heartache and sorrow, it would be a stretch to think that its substance would not have a negative effect on the rest of the tree of her life.

Richard Andrew King

PRINCESS DIANA & MARILYN MONROE: SIMILARITIES

The lives of Princess Diana and Marilyn Monroe were very similar in general terms. Both were beautiful women in search of love; both had unhappy childhoods, fame beyond belief, multiple romantic heartaches, marriages to famous men, adoration from the multitudes, paparazzi pressure beyond compare, mysterious liaisons, tragic deaths, short lives and legacies of renown reserved only for a rare few.

What is even more interesting is that, numerologically, their very public, luminous lives were extremely interwoven and, in many ways, mirrors. This would be expected logically because, as we're seeing in the lives of our featured icons, like numbers generate like results.

Both Marilyn Monroe and Princess Diana had 7 Lifepaths, 4 Expressions and 2 PEs. They both had the numbers 5 and 7 in their Challenges; 1-4-5 and 8 in their Pinnacles, and both had an 8 void in their name.

Marilyn and Diana were also born on the 1st of a month beginning with the letter J (Marilyn on 1 June; Diana on 1 July); both died tragically under mysterious circumstances in the month of August (the 8th calendar month: remember the 8 void in their charts?) at the age of 36 while in their 2nd Pinnacle/Challenge period, and both ladies had 19 letters in their birth names, creating an 8 challenge subcap with a 1 addcap theme! It is no wonder their fates were similar. Similar energies produce similar results. It is the science of life. One plus One make Two, not Three. Thus, Marilyn Monroe and Princess Diana were practically sisters (at least in the vibrational sense).

PRINCESS DIANA: MASTER NUMBERS

Diana did not have as many master numbers in her chart as some of our other featured individuals. Still, the ones she had are powerful, especially the double 55-1s and 33-6s.

Master Numbers in Princess Diana's Chart	
11	Life PE Material Nature 2nd Epoch PE 4th (Crown) Challenge PE
22	Nature 3rd (Grand) Challenge 4th (Crown) Pinnacle PE
33	*Spencer* Name Timeline PE (double)
44	none
55	*Frances* Name Timeline PE (double) Fairytale Wedding to Prince Charles (29 July 1981)
66	none
77	none
88	none
99	none

Richard Andrew King

MARRIAGE & DEATH YEARS

Diana married Prince Charles on 29 July 1981 at age 20. This was in the second "A" of "Diana" and generated a 1/8v Letter Timeline IR set. As fate would have it, Diana died on 31 August 1996 during the "A" of "Frances" which also generated a 1/8v LTL IR set. Here is evidence of the 1/8v creating a beginning (her fairytale marriage to a prince) that was to experience disconnections and heartache (remember the 1 passed through the 7 to create the 8 void) and an ending—literally of her life, also manifested in a 1/8 voided IR set. Such is the power of numbers and their reality.

Prince Charles, Princess Diana, Nancy Regan, President Ronald Regan
November, 1985

(Photo courtesy of Wikimedia Commons)

SUMMARY

There can be no question that Princess Diana was an exceptional human being who led an extraordinary life. To say otherwise would be to be blind. She was the most photographed, the most written about, the most talked about, the most famous woman of her time. Her life was exceedingly public, more so perhaps than even she desired. It had fairytale dreams come true. It had nightmares. There was happiness, especially with her children. And, of course, there was the immense sorrow, the sadness, the pain, the suffering, the tragedy, the tears.

Diana was an English aristocratic girl child who suffered throughout her life from the fact that she was not the boy-child her parents wished for, with no outstanding qualities other than her innocent desire to love others and be loved by them, who became a Royal Princess, the Mother of kings and Patroness of Britain's future and who, after being stripped of her worldly royal title by a queen, became a Queen. . . of Hearts and, in an all-too-painful process, one of the greatest icons in English history. How fortunate she was not born a boy! *The King's Book of Numerology, Volume 9: Numeric Biography, Princess Diana* details her life in full from a numerological basis.

Some of the interesting components in the numerology chart of Princess Diana are . . .

- The 5/9 Grand Pinnacle/Challenge Couplet
- Diana's 9/22-4 Crown Pinnacle of rulership, power and wealth
- The 7/11-2v Crown Challenge revealing stress in relationship
- Her double $55-1^2$ Name Timeline PE of *Frances*
- Her double $33-6^2$ Name Timeline PE of *Spencer*
- Her 1/5 1st Epoch and 6/1 1st Challenge reflecting difficult issues in the home life, with males and with her own sense of security

PRINCESS DIANA – QUOTES

Being a princess isn't all it's cracked up to be.

I'd like to be a queen in people's hearts but I don't see myself being queen of this country.

It's vital that the monarchy keeps in touch with the people. It's what I try and do.

Richard Andrew King

Only do what your heart tells you.

Family is the most important thing in the world.

I live for my sons. I would be lost without them.

I want my boys to have an understanding of people's emotions, their insecurities, people's distress, and their hopes and dreams.

Any sane person would have left long ago. But I cannot. I have my sons.

I wear my heart on my sleeve.

Life is just a journey.

Hugs can do great amounts of good - especially for children.

I don't go by the rule book . . . I lead from the heart, not the head.

I will fight for my children on any level so they can reach their potential as human beings and in their public duties.

What must it be like for a little boy to read that daddy never loved mummy?

I want to walk into a room, be it a hospital for the dying or a hospital for the sick children, and feel that I am needed. I want to do, not just to be.

If you find someone you love in your life, then hang on to that love.

The biggest disease this day and age is that of people feeling unloved.

Anywhere I see suffering, that is where I want to be, doing what I can.

I knew what my job was; it was to go out and meet the people and love them.

I like to be a free spirit. Some don't like that, but that's the way I am.

Carry out a random act of kindness, with no expectation of reward, safe in the knowledge that one day someone might do the same for you.

Everyone of us needs to show how much we care for each other and, in the process, care for ourselves.

There were three of us in this marriage, so it was a bit crowded.

I think like any marriage, especially when you've had divorced parents like myself, you want to try even harder to make it work.

The greatest problem in the world today is intolerance. Everyone is so intolerant of each other.

I don't want expensive gifts; I don't want to be bought. I have everything I want. I just want someone to be there for me, to make me feel safe and secure.

Richard Andrew King

QUEEN OF HEARTS

© Richard Andrew King

Mirror, mirror, on the wall,

what can we learn

from the rise and fall

of a tear-laden princess

of the royal arts,

who traded her crown

for a Queen of Hearts?

A tender child of tender years

whose need for love had turned to tears

in the wake of her parent's failing joy,

lamenting a girl and wishing a boy.

Such was the omen.

Frightful start - beginning life

with a wounded heart;

tender passions torn and worn;

unfaithful mother; bitter scorn;

endless nights of endless fears;

little brother's sea of tears -

crying, weeping, no mummy home;

big sister's cross - to walk alone.

The flower blossomed,

sweet youth in Spring;

betrothed a prince

who would be king.

The marriage bargain -

fairytale dream

for a tarnished crown

and a faithless ring.

Mirror, mirror, on the wall,

what can we learn

from the rise and fall

of a Princess hounded by a press,

void of manners and relentless;

stalking, never caring, forever blind

to the human need for some peace of mind;

for a little space; for a little breath?

Shameful, sinful, flashbulb death.

Mirror, mirror, in the sky,

faithful lovers question why;

young and lovely; future bright;

stolen dreams; fateful night.

Why such a Princess loved by all

should reap the Whirlwind and the Fall?

Mirror, mirror, in the night,

reflect a star whose beacon light

shone 'round the world

to hush a cry;

now shines forever

in a royal sky.

Excerpt from

The King's Book of Numerology, Volume 9: Numeric Biography – Princess Diana
and *Blueprint of a Princess*

Richard Andrew King

HISTORIC ICON #12

SARAH PALIN

Born: Sarah Louise Heath – 11 February 1964

----

* 1st woman and youngest person elected Governor of Alaska

* 1st Republican woman nominated for the Vice-Presidency

of the United States of America

* Best selling author

(State of Alaska Official Portraits - Jeff Schultz)

Buck up or stay in the truck.

You know what they say the difference

between a hockey mom and a pit bull is? Lipstick.

Richard Andrew King

Sarah Palin is a powerhouse personality, political figure, media commentator and best-selling author. She is independent, courageous, strong, forthright and attractive. She is pro-life, pro America, pro individual responsibility. She has the kind of backbone and grit that made America great. In the opinion of many people, Sarah Palin is a true American who promotes American values and idealism.

Unquestionably, Sarah Palin has power. When an individual authors a book which becomes a #1 Best Seller *before* it is released to the public, that is power. When an individual writes a few comments on a Twitter page and ignites commentary from a nation, that is power. When an individual draws ruthlessly negative comments from her adversaries, even derisive insults directed toward her special needs child, that is definitely power. Whether Sarah Palin is revered or reviled, one thing is undeniable—Sarah Palin is an American original, an independent thinker and . . . a powerhouse in lipstick.

Margaret Thatcher, who served as Prime Minister of Great Britain from 1979 to 1990, was known as the "Iron Lady" for her tough demeanor. One of her famous quotes is: *If you want to cut your own throat, don't come to me for a bandage.* In other words, be accountable, take responsibility for your own actions and don't look to others to fix what you break or make better what you make worse.

Sarah Palin is much a cut of the same cloth of personal accountability when she says, *Buck up or stay in the truck.* It's tough talk from a tough, strong and courageous woman. All leaders take stands. Otherwise they wouldn't be leaders. Sarah Palin is a leader. She's proven it, and her destiny not only has called her to it but demands it.

PROVOCATIVE QUESTIONS

- What numbers define Sarah Palin's leadership fate?
- What master number reflects Palin's *Going Rogue* persona?
- What IR set indicates Palin's public power?
- What is unique about all of Sarah Palin's Challenges?
- What is unique about Palin's Epochs?

- What single number dominates Palin's chart?
- Which master number reflects her communicative ability?

LEADERSHIP & *GOING ROGUE* PERSONA

No master number reflects the *Going Rogue* persona more than the 55-1. This occupies the Material Soul and Material Nature of Sarah Palin. Not only does she desire to be a maverick and do things her own way, it is also her personality to do so. When one of the Soul energies match either the Nature, Material Nature, Expression or PE, it finds release and its energies are strengthened and intensified. Sarah Palin will always do things her own way. She's a rebel, a revolutionary. She can't be controlled. She is independent, free-thinking and she's going to live up to her ideals, energy and destiny. Certainly, the double 55-1 in her Basic Matrix is a key component of her identity.

Basic Matrix: Sarah Louise Heath (Sarah Palin)

LP	Exp.	PE	Soul	MS	Nature	MN	Voids
33-6	8	77-5	4	55-1	22-4	55-1	4-7
Note: 33 in her 3rd House of Communication							

The number 1 also occupies every one of her Epoch PE positions. Take a look at her Life Matrix.

Richard Andrew King

LIFE MATRIX
Voids: 4 & 7
SARAH LOUISE HEATH
11 FEBRUARY 1964

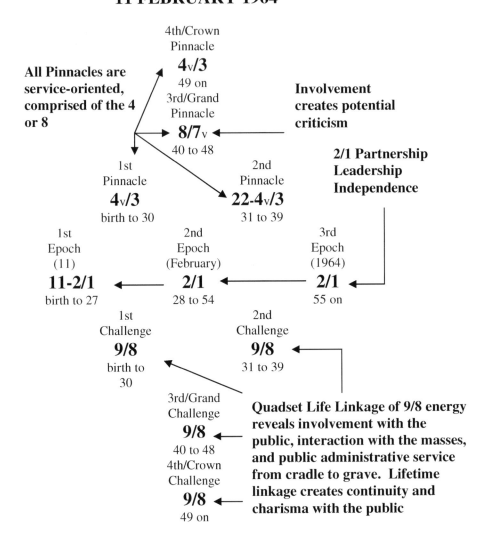

All Pinnacles are service-oriented, comprised of the 4 or 8

4th/Crown Pinnacle
4v/3
49 on

3rd/Grand Pinnacle
8/7v
40 to 48

Involvement creates potential criticism

1st Pinnacle
4v/3
birth to 30

2nd Pinnacle
22-4v/3
31 to 39

2/1 Partnership Leadership Independence

1st Epoch (11)
11-2/1
birth to 27

2nd Epoch (February)
2/1
28 to 54

3rd Epoch (1964)
2/1
55 on

1st Challenge
9/8
birth to 30

2nd Challenge
9/8
31 to 39

3rd/Grand Challenge
9/8
40 to 48

4th/Crown Challenge
9/8
49 on

Quadset Life Linkage of 9/8 energy reveals involvement with the public, interaction with the masses, and public administrative service from cradle to grave. Lifetime linkage creates continuity and charisma with the public

Notice the 2/1 IR set in her 1st, 2nd and 3rd Epoch. This indicates herself, leadership and action (1) resulting from partnership, relationship and others (2). The 2/1 IR set exists from birth to death. Palin cannot escape being a leader.

The Four 9/8 Challenges

As we see from her Life Matrix, all four of Sarah Palin's Challenges are a 9/8. This means that for her entire life—from cradle to grave—she will be managing the same energies of public (9) interaction and connection (8). This 9/8 Influence/Reality set (see *The King's Book of Numerology II: Forecasting - Part 1*) is what gives Palin her enormous public appeal, magnetism and charisma.

The number 9, the *Grand Elemental*, represents all people. Therefore, every Challenge position will place Sarah Palin among the masses. When the 9 filters through her 8 Expression, the result is an 8 of interaction, connection, involvement, management and administration on the public stage and in public service. It is this 9/8 IR set that is a major player in Sarah Palin's public magnetism and success. Furthermore, the 9/8 IR set doubles with the 2/1 IR sets in her Epochs. This creates a double Life Linkage for Sarah Palin in the arena of the public, universal stage, others, management and leadership.

The power of this 9/8 Influence/Reality set cannot be underestimated. No two numbers together are more charismatic, magnetic and socially powerful than the 9 and the 8 together. 9 rules. 8 connects. A person may have this combination at some time in his or her life but it is very, very rare for a person to have it present in every Challenge position for the entire life. What this means is that Sarah Palin's popularity with the masses is neither a fluke nor short lived, and any adversary should be very wary because Palin's popularity is an intrinsic part of her life's blueprint. Because this 9/8 combination is in her Challenge position, she will—as is evident—be both revered and reviled. Such is the duality of this creation. Every coin has two sides; every energy reflects both a positive and negative aspect. By natural law, it cannot be otherwise.

The 8 Influence

The number 8 strengthens Sarah Palin's chart in other ways than being a part of her 9/8 Challenge Life Linkage. Notice her Expression in her Basic Matrix? It's an 8. Sarah Palin, i.e., *Sarah Louise Heath*, is the personal embodiment of involvement, connection, interaction, orchestration, administration, management, social power and being in-the-loop of society. Her very being manifests these qualities.

Richard Andrew King

There's more. Notice her Grand Pinnacle? It is also an 8. It is located in the very center of her 6 Lifepath of love, nurturing, compassion, community.

There's still more. Look at the PE in her Name Timeline of *Sarah*. Not only is it an 8, it is a 44-8—the number of generalship, leadership, command.

Name Timeline (NTL): Sarah Louise Heath			
	First	Middle	Last
Names	Sarah	Louise	Heath
Timeline	birth to 20	21 to 47	48 to 71
General	20	27	24
IR Set	2	9	6
	8	6	3
Master #s	44	33	66

We're not done. Count the Hs in her birth name, *Sarah Louise Heath*. There are three—more energy of management and involvement. All together, Palin has a *Decaset* (set of 10) of the number 8 in her King's Numerology™ chart—Expression, Grand Pinnacle, NTL PE of *Sarah*, quadset PE in her Challenges and triset of Hs in her natal name. Having ten of any number is massive. Her decaset of 8s throughout her chart, and therefore throughout her life, reveal a person whose entire life is awash with the energy of management, leadership and command. As a single number, 8 dominates Palin's chart.

COMMUNICATION POWER

Sarah Palin's personal and public power are greatly enhanced by the master communicator 33-6 energy in four different places in her chart:

- Lifepath
- 3rd House of Communication
- Name Timeline PE of *Louise*
- Letter Timeline PE in the "I" of *Louise*

The Lifepath is the script of a person's life. It defines those things the actor (the Expression) must perform to create a role (the PE). The Lifepath can also be seen as the energy world into which a person is born. Palin's simple Lifepath is a 6—the energy of the family, whether that family is a personal home, community home, national home or planetary home. The 6 nurtures, loves and takes care of those in his or her environment.

The 33 as a master root of the 6 emits powerful energies of words, communication, art, expression, health, beauty, children. Palin's special needs child is a reflection, to some degree, of her Lifepath of the 6 and its nurturing qualities. But the same energy she applies to her children and family are also the same ones she applies to her community, whether local or national. It's not uncommon for leaders or presidents to have 33-6 in their charts because it is through words and communication that people are moved to action. Indeed, the pen is mightier than the sword, and the pen is nothing more than the tool used to communicate words and ideas. Great leaders such as Abraham Lincoln, George Washington, John F. Kennedy, Winston Churchill and Mother Teresa all had 33-6 in their charts.

Sarah Palin also has the 33 in her 3rd House of Communication. This is more communicative power. The 3rd House is the house of communication, and to have the master number of communication—the 33-6—in the 3rd House is dynamite.

Palin's middle name *Louise* also houses a 33-6 PE. Furthermore, the "I" of *Louise* also carries a 33-6 PE. All of these 33-6 components in Palin's chart create a quadset of potent communication ability. For confirmation of this, one need look no further than her address before the 2008 Republican National Convention in Saint Paul, Minnesota. Sarah Palin brought the house down and showed her ability to speak eloquently before the nation. It was an impressive demonstration of a person's communicative power—a direct manifestation of her 33-6 quadset.

The 66-3

The 33-6 is further aided by her 66-3 NTL PE in the name of *Heath*. She moves into this energy field on her birthday in 2012. It lasts for twenty-four years, from age 48 to 71. The difference between the 33-6 and the 66-3 is that the former is love of community, country and responsibility

Richard Andrew King

(6) based in words and self-expression (33), while the later is words (3) based in love, compassion, community, country, responsibility (66).

AMERICA, SARAH PALIN AND THE NUMBERS 5

Palin's Life Performance (PE): 77-5

The PE or Performance/Experience component of a numerology chart shows the reality of the individual (Expression) reading a script (Lifepath) and giving a performance (PE). In effect, the PE is the role a person will play on the great life stage. Palin's 77-5 PE indicates diversity, versatility, change (5) built on reflection, thought, analysis, study (7). The 5 is the number of freedom, which is also America's Lifepath and Material Soul. This 5 connection means Palin exemplifies the American philosophy of freedom and independence. This 5 therefore creates a natural affinity between the Soul and Lifepath of America and Palin's role in life. America has a 5 Material Soul. She wants to be free. It is her driving passion. She also has a 5 Lifepath, so her life lessons also focus on freedom in both its positive and negative aspects. In effect, what America wants in her heart-of-hearts, from the depth of her soul, is the role Sarah Palin is giving in her life . . . freedom.

Another characteristic of the 5 is that it is the fulcrum or midpoint of the Alpha-Numeric spectrum of single numbers between 1 through 9. The number 5 is the *Number of Man* because we humans have 5 in common more than any other number – five toes on each foot, five fingers on each hand, thirty-two teeth (3 + 2 =5), five common senses, 5 rings on the Olympic flag, 365 days in a year (3 + 6 + 5 = 14 > 1 + 4 = 5). Therefore, it is exceptionally easy for Sarah Palin to move up and down the scale of numbers, and since people can be identified by numbers, that means she can move easily among the masses. This 5 aspect to her chart works in concert with her 9s, thus strengthening her public and universal appeal.

CRITICS AND ACRIMONY: THE 8/7 GRAND PINNACLE

When anyone flies above the radar, is outspoken, has courage and opinions and does not back down from a fight or cower at the onslaught of her adversary's criticism, ridicule, taunting or disparagement, that person is usually attacked more fiercely. Sarah Palin's strength and public appeal have drawn criticism and acrimony from some people, basically those opposed to her political platform; some have been vicious and totally untoward, even pathetically stooping to attack her special needs Down Syndrome child.

Is this in her numbers? Yes. Palin's Grand Pinnacle is an 8/7. This is a combination that can result in criticism as depicted by the 7 PE which, as we have seen in the charts of many of the featured individuals in this work, creates turmoil, trouble, concern and chaos to some degree or another. It is no different for Sarah Palin. Laws of life favor no one. We are all bound by the same laws and the number 7 in an outcome position can certainly create turmoil. In a fuller ciphering the 8/7 becomes 8/(8)/16-7, thus depicting the *Great Purifier* 16-7 energy.

MASTER NUMBERS IN SARAH PALIN'S CHART

Sarah Palin has every master number in her chart except the 88 and 99. Most notable are the quadstack of 33-6 and the double stack of 55-1 (following page).

Master Numbers in Sarah Palin's Chart	
11	1st Epoch Letter Timeline PE in the "E" of *Louise* Letter Timeline PE in the "E" of *Heath*
22	Nature 2nd Pinnacle
33	Lifepath 3rd House of Communication Name Timeline PE of *Louise* Letter Timeline PE in the "I" of *Louise*
44	Name Timeline PE of *Sarah*
55	Material Soul Material Nature
66	Name Timeline PE of *Heath*
77	Life Performance/Experience (PE)
88	none
99	none

SUMMARY

Sarah Palin is a powerhouse in lipstick; of this there is no doubt. Furthermore, as with all of us, her destiny is contained within the numbers of her King's Numerology[tm] chart, and that destiny is saturated with energies of interaction and connection with the public, service, work, devotion, security, communication, inspiration, originality, action and leadership.

Some of the interesting components in the numerology chart of Sarah Palin are . . .

- Quadset (four) of 33-6 Master Communicator energy in her Lifepath, 3rd House of Communication, Name Timeline PE of *Louise*, Letter Timeline PE in the "I" of *Louise*
- Double stack of 55-1 energy in her Material Soul and Material Nature
- A 77-5 Master number in her Performance/Experience (role of her life) resonating with America's Soul and Lifepath
- Decaset (10) of 8 energy in her Expression, Name Timeline PE of *Sarah*, Core Pinnacle, quadset in her Challenge PEs and triset of Letter Timeline PEs in the "Hs" of *Sarah* and *Heath*
- A Life Challenge structure of only 9/8 energy occupying her entire life from cradle to grave
- Double life linkage in her 2/1 Epochs and 9/8 Challenges

SARAH PALIN – QUOTES

Here's a little newsflash for those reporters and commentators: I'm not going to Washington to seek their good opinion. I'm going to Washington to serve this great country.

Buck up or stay in the truck.

You know what they say the difference between a hockey mom and a pit bull is? Lipstick.

Richard Andrew King

My fellow citizens, the American Presidency is not supposed to be a journey of personal discovery.

We don't need to fundamentally transform America. We need to restore America.

America's finest – our men and women in uniform, are a force for good throughout the world, and that is nothing to apologize for.

I'm just one of many moms who will say an extra prayer each night for our sons and daughters going into harm's way.

Americans expect us to go to Washington for the right reason, and not just to mingle with the right people.

We need American sources of resources, we need American energy, brought to you by American ingenuity and produced by American workers.

Sometimes even the greatest joys bring challenge, and children with special needs inspire a very, very special love.

I'm pro-life. I'll do all I can to see every baby is created with a future and potential.

The fact that drilling won't solve every problem is no excuse to do nothing at all.

To reduce deficit spending and our enormous debt, you reign in spending. You cut the budget. You don't take more from the private sector and grow government with it.

POWER, FAME & KINGS

Richard Andrew King

THE CAUTION OF POWER

© 2009 by Richard Andrew King

Be ever careful of your power
in the hour of your glory.
Be ever careful of your arrogance
in the instance of your reign.
In a karmic world ever temporal,
your greatness is ephemeral,
and any abuses of your crown
will, unfailingly, circle back 'round to you again!

Therefore, dear friend, take the highest road
but seek the lowest ground;
restrain the reins of your renown.
Be always humble, never proud;
do not, yourself, speak aloud
your fame or name or temporal power
as you rejoice within your tower.
Best let others shower you
with the rains of your acclaim.

All beg and pray for power and fame,
but few assess the heinous flames of same.
Their power blinds them.
Thus, they never heed
the dangers lurking in the Weeds of Rank,
and they forget as they go 'round,
"Uneasy lies the head that wears a crown."
As light to dark and back again,
so circle fully acts of sin.

Richard Andrew King

Thus, be cautious in your power

as you regale in your tower.

Note those below and shower them

with all the glory that's in Him,

for He and He alone is King,

and He and He alone will bring

to you His Blessèd Power

and save you from the Devil's Tower

as you go 'round and 'round again.

FAME'S ORDAINED

© Richard Andrew King

Fact is often stranger
than fiction we create;
more absolute and resolute
than laws we legislate.

The facts of life cry out
their veracity to proclaim
one's health and wealth and struggles,
and surely that of fame,
are secretly embedded within our
birthdate and our name.

Yes, fact is often stranger
than truths we do revere,
or the spooks and kooks and goblins
we have come to fear,

but have no doubt Reality,
its lifeblood unrestrained,
will extricate the ignorance
and ardently proclaim
this simple fact of life:
"Fame's Ordained."

Richard Andrew King

KINGDOMS & KINGS

© Richard Andrew King

Kingdoms and kings, cultures and queens,

all rise and fall by Karmic Law.

Celebrities and nobodies,

Heroes and heroines,

Princes and paupers,

cheers and sneers,

the high and low

all bow before

the King

who rules

not by committee,

popularity or notoriety,

but by Divine Decree.

Uneasy truly lies the head that wears a crown,

and egos overblown will surely drown

under the weight of their

glorified presumption

and consumption.

- So -

let it be known that ultimately

what was reaped was sewn,

and that a self-appointed

and anointed crown

will only drown

the head of

him who

wears

it.

Richard Andrew King

APPENDIX – KEYWORDS

EXPANDED KEYWORDS/KEY PHRASE CHART

Note 1: every number maintains a positive and negative side (polarity), just as every coin has two sides. Furthermore, we cannot hold a coin without holding both sides simultaneously. The same is true for numbers and our lives reflect both the positive and negative aspects of each vibration to some degree. In other words, no number is perfect, no chart is perfect, no human being is perfect. We all have assets and liabilities, good karmas and bad karmas.

Note 2: every single number has ten binary or two-digit numbers attached to it and which, when added together reduce to form that specific single number.

Note 3: it would be impossible to list every word in the English language which is attached to each of the nine basic numbers. After all, there are only nine basic numbers and hundreds of thousands of words. Therefore, a complete keyword list would be impossible to generate. Below, however, are more words and phrases than simply those used in the basic keyword chart.

Note 4: if voided in a chart, especially if a voided challenge occurs, the influences can be quite negative, reflecting the dark side of a number.

ONE - 1
(Fire) (Symbols: Sun, Staff)

10	19	28	37	46	55	64	73	82	91

The Primal Force, first cause, yang, fire, vitality, action, man, male, masculine, father, self, identity, creativity, ego, skill, individual, self-confidence, boss, leader, director, doer, initiator, creator, authority figure, pioneer, star, center of attention, willpower, self-control, independence, self-sufficiency, determination, activates, initiates, creates, dominates, leads, attains, driving, strong, courageous, powerful, dynamic, decisive, unbending, steadfast, dominant, linear, single-minded, unique, original, starts, new beginnings, creation, genesis, assertive, aggressive, overbearing, self-indulgent, ego-maniacal, selfish, self-obsessed, tom-boy, rational, reasonable, logical, unemotional, radiating, initiating, purpose, direction. TIME FRAME: a time of initiation, initiating, action, seed planting, new beginnings, starts; a period of the self and its attainments; being accountable and responsible; being the leader or bread-winner; issues of identity, self-worth, males and all things Yang; moving ahead; getting new direction; planting flags; solo excursions; tests of courage and standing alone against all people and all odds. Ones make things happen.

Richard Andrew King

TWO - 2
(Water) (Symbols: Moon, Scales, Twin Towers)

11	20	29	38	47	56	65	74	83	92

Yin, water, woman, female, feminine, mother, others, relationships, especially those that are close, personal and intimate; 2s take sides, support, separate, helper, assistant, adversary, adversity, adversarial, assistance, follower, dependent, diplomatic, cooperative, cooperation, collaboration, consideration, teamwork, passive, patient, non-obtrusive, intuitive, receptive, responsive, agreeable, amenable, affable, kind, warm, devoted, sweet, gentle-hearted, peacemaking, harmonizing, equalizing, submissive, rhythmic, equalizing, equilibrium, competition, rivalry, contention, confliction, duality, duplicity, deceit, indecisive, division, the great divide, 'us vs. them,' intuitive, behind the scenes, bending, yielding, non-assertive, together, taking sides, opposition, vacillation, irrational, illogical, unreasonable, emotional, reflecting (as in the Moon reflecting light, water reflecting an image) and absorbing (vs. radiating of the 1), acquiescing. TIME FRAME: a period of others, serving them, being helpful and supportive; being the helper, partner, team player, opponent, adversary, inhibitor, diplomat, judge, arbitrator, go-between; lessons of tolerance and intolerance; a time of all things Yin; period of competition, stress, adversarial conditions, tensions, tug-o-wars; learning to get along; being balanced; finding the middle path; being deceptive or dealing with deception and/or the interference or inhibition of others and either their helpfulness or hindering; a time of high energy and friction.

THREE - 3
(Air) (Symbols: Triangle, Trident)

12	21	30	39	48	57	66	75	84	93

Trinity, triads, air, the triangle (Ancient symbol of Perfection), The Golden Mean of Aristotle, Yin and Yang in perfect balance (the symbol of the Tao), art, artistry, artistic, image (moving or still), fashion, words, communication, expression, personal integration, fulfillment, complete approach to health, happiness, wholeness, holiness, holistic, well-being, marriage, joy, enjoyment, pleasure, parties, friends, good times, talkative, verbal, gregarious, approachable, gossip, social, outgoing, fun-loving, entertaining, light-hearted, vibrant, alive, creative, imaginative, happy, optimistic, cheerful, charming, health, beauty, vanity, writing, acting, performing, glamorous, ease, disease, dis-ease, hostility, poisonous words, harsh, critical, stern, harsh, vain, egotistical; often found in charts of politicians. TIME FRAME: a time of self-expression and fulfillment, being creative, using words, being involved with health, beauty, disease, dis-ease, acting, writing, painting, modeling, sculpting; a time of children and seeking perfection and balance; a time of happiness (if positively aspected) and unhappiness and harshness (if negatively aspected); can give a sense of entitlement or ease of life coming toward the self; issues of purity, holiness, unholiness, pure pleasure or debauchery, harshness and communication which is either uplifting or destructive. It is a time of integration and self-realization, a time where the goodness or meanness of life will reveal itself; a time of happiness and/or sadness; pleasure and/or pain.

FOUR - 4
(Earth) (Symbols: Square, Roots, Anchors, Chains)

13	22	31	40	49	58	67	76	85	94

Earth, order, structure, framework, form, foundation, boundaries, rules, regulations, guidelines, routine, status quo, concrete, confines, confinements, proprieties, mechanics, work, service, servant, matter, materialism, transformation, transmutation, security, stability, effort, hard, stubborn, recalcitrant, resistance, resistant, confinement, toil, physical strength, solid power, steadfast, sturdy, the rock, anchor, roots, chains, obstacles, tradition, convention, duty, loyalty, dependability, discipline, control, commitment, construction, prudent, clerical, industrious, down to earth, frugal, practical, organizing, house, beams, foundations, constancy, regimentation, classification, organization, organized, systemize, non-adventurous, predictable, obstinate, boring, routine, patterns, status quo, plodding along, unchanging, the order of things, events, situations, circumstances and relationships; if voided or challenged can be unstable, unfaithful, dishonest, weak, insecure, faithless. TIME FRAME: a time of work, effort, restriction (especially in conjunction with 5 energy), limitation, grinding it out, being consistent, not changing, conforming, nuts & bolts; a time when the focus is on the structures of life - financial, moral, ethical, routines, regimes, order, discipline; it is a time of learning about boundaries and borders, rules and regulations, service and work, faithfulness and devotion, sacrifice and surrender.

FIVE - 5
(Fire) (Symbols: Wings, Wheels, Needles, Broken Chains)

14	23	32	41	50	59	68	77	86	95

Free, freedom, fire, change, movement, detachment, detaching, shifting, wild, wayward, careless, adventure, adventurous, roam, roaming, liberation, liberate, unrestrained, undisciplined, unsettled, non-restriction, nonrestrictive, shifts, slavery mercurial, spontaneous, excitement, experience, experiential, variety, talent, versatility, people, senses, sexuality, sensations, stimulation, motion, energy, mercurial, multi-faceted, many sided, assortment, exuberant, enthusiastic, exciting, spontaneous, foot-loose, flamboyant, dashing, energetic, exploring, exposure, exhibitionist, adventurous, travel, unpredictable, unconventional, uncertain, unstable, instability, the crowd, diverse, diversity, letting go, free-spirited, rebellious, liberation, liberating, stimulating, stimulants, non-complacent, temptation, temperance, restraint, indulgence, animated, exuberant, flamboyant, volatile. TIME FRAME: a time of freedom, change, shifting, movement, uncertainty, detachment, letting go, releasing, wiping out the old, exploring, investigating, experimenting, sexuality, sensual gratification; temperance and fidelity challenged; not a time to cling, but a time to let go, detach, release and move on; also a time testing our true understanding of freedom which is not action devoid of consequence but action taken in consideration of consequence, action taken in pursuit of sensual pleasures, sense gratification and wild sorties into the realms of indulgence create slavery and bondage and all the suffering, woes and wailings associated with such incarceration, action of freedom taken in consideration of consequence by following the inner voice of conscience, temperance and restraint, the end result will be true freedom and liberation from sensual enslavement. The key note during a Five period is to be wise; look ahead to the results of your actions; exercise moderation and fidelity and do not step into the regions of material indulgence.

SIX - 6
(Water) (Symbol: Heart)

15	24	33	42	51	60	69	78	87	96

Love, hate, home, water, hearth, matters of the heart, romance, domesticity, adjustability, responsibility, accountability, personal love, art, artistic, beauty, community, harmonious, caring, warm, nurturing, understanding, soft, comfortable, dependable, conscientious, kind, responsive, protective, protecting, music, sex, singing, harmonizing, hatred, cruelty, family discord, family issues and concerns, addiction, jealousy, envy, resentment. TIME FRAME: a time of matters of the heart, love issues, domestic (individual, personal, community, national, global) energies, concerns, responsibilities, possible addictions, romance, lust, sexuality.

SEVEN - 7
(Air) (Symbols: Hurricane, Thinker, Cross)

16	25	34	43	52	61	70	79	88	97

Spirit, spiritual, mystical, meticulous, air, bliss, chaos, thought, the thinker, introspection, perception, investigation, inquisition, intuition, reflection, examination, judgment, recession, repose, receding, distancing, counseling, alienation, study, testing, reflecting, evaluating, reviewing, learning, processing, isolation, isolated, solitary, solitude, separate, separation, seclusion, secrecy, privacy, analysis, religion, rest, quiet, calm, peace, tranquility, inwardness, the 'within', perfection, poise, wisdom, saints/sinners, light/dark, curious, distant, cool, cold, removed, withdrawn, shy, reclusive, alone, lonely, loneliness, refined, non-social, purification, stressed, distressed, troubled, turmoil, torment, tumult, trauma, unworldly, considerate, inconsiderate, cold, cruel, calculating, harsh, ruthless, brutal thoughtful, thoughtless, private, secret, secretive, stealthy, hide, hidden, investigative, trouble, problems, worry, concern, anxiety, anxious, scandal, scandalous, misery, miserable, grief, deep, despair, anguish, chaos, chaotic, distressful, soul-searching, cynical, cynicism. TIME FRAME: a time for the building of inner strength and developing the inner self and all things spiritual; a time of being alone; a time of testing; a time of reflecting, analyzing, studying, teaching, pondering, going within and searching, asking questions and seeking answers, becoming mature through the fires of the heart and emotions, being brought to our knees in humble supplication of the power of God, Source, Spirit, the Lord; the time of the hurricane; choices of fidelity or adultery; peace or chaos; a time of purification by fire; a time to float across to the other side on a river of your own tears; the time to find and cling to God.

EIGHT - 8
(Earth) (Symbol: Lemniscate)

17	26	35	44	53	62	71	80	89	98

Earth sign, interaction, involvement, connection, disconnection, orchestration, coordination, manipulation, administration, circulation, association, associating, continuation, continuity, opportunity, responsive, (non-responsive if void), mixing, karmic conduit, circuits, circulate, systems, worldly success-power-wealth, opportunist, materialism, material comfort, management, marketing, promotion, commerce, business, flow, efficiency of motion-movement-management, being in the loop, administrator, executive, coordinating, socialization, socializing, external power, leadership, organization, involve, engage, usury, social importance and power, externalization, the 'without,' can also reference a lack of understanding of 'give and take' and 'cause and consequence.' TIME FRAME: a time of connection/disconnection, interaction, management, procrastination (if negatively afflicted), marketing, making business contacts, socializing, organizing and administrating, executing as one who is an executive; a time of association, administration, manipulation, orchestration, circulation, coordination; a time of bringing things together and making it happen; a time to be careful of using others to our advantage; a time of success or failure where all things work together harmoniously (for success) or fall apart to create failure.

NINE - 9
(Grand Elemental - All Elements) (Symbol: Crown)

18	27	36	45	54	63	72	81	90	99

Universality, timeless, macrocosm, endings, conclusions, completions, climaxes, chameleon, volunteer, inclusions, humanitarian, humanitarianism, teacher, impersonal love, broadcast, broadcaster, broadcasting, public exposure, pushy, magnanimous, regal, royal, philanthropic, philosophical, all encompassing, understanding, generous, tolerant, broad-minded, global, worldly, strong, dominant, domineering, controlling, artistic, intense emotion, acting, theatrical, charismatic, travel, the 'many,' healer, healing, the universal giver, expansion, the world, represents the universal languages of music, art, love. TIME FRAME: a time of conclusions, endings, resolutions, terminations, finalizations, volunteering, being public and being in the public eye and spotlight; moving within the macrocosm and life stage, moving among the masses, being famous or infamous; a time of travel - mentally or physically; a time of higher education and the advancement of thought and philosophy; a time to be universal and far-reaching; a time to be the great communicator, the powerful ruler, the icon of a culture; a time to serve humanity and expand one's thought beyond the finite boundaries of the self; a time to act, expand and be known. It is life stage for theater, medicine, sport and war; strong, even dominant personality and persona, possibly including or bordering on being over-bearing, domineering, imperious.

Richard Andrew King

GLOSSARY

Addcap	A number derived through the vertical addition of numbers in a group
Albert Einstein	19th/20th Century German-born theoretical physicist; regarded as the father of modern physics
Aleister Crowley	19th/20th Century English astrologer and occultist
Alpha Numeric Spectrum	The scale representing the single numbers 1 through 9
Amelia Earhart	20th Century American aviatrix
Artistic Triad	The combination of the numbers 3, 6 and 9
Baruch de Spinoza	17th Century Dutch philosopher
Basic Matrix	A general numeric profile of a person and his destiny comprised of eight components, each component identified by a number or numbers
Benjamin Disraeli	19th Century British Prime Minister and statesman
Bible	Holy book of the Christian religion
Biset	Numerical combination of two single numbers, number combinations or number patterns
Bistack	Simultaneous numerical combination of two numbers, number combinations or number patterns
Challenge #1	The Life Matrix number derived by subtraction of the day and month of birth
Challenge #2	The Life Matrix number derived by subtraction of the month and year of birth
Challenge #3	The Life Matrix number derived by subtraction of Challenges 1 & 2; known as the Grand Challenge; it is one-half of the core/center of a person's life; the other half is the Grand Pinnacle
Challenge #4	The Life Matrix number derived by subtraction of the day and year of birth
Challenges	The four parts of the Life Matrix derived by subtraction; denotes challenges, difficulties, and places in one's life demanding focus
Charan Singh	20th Century saint and mystic
Charles Kuhl	Charles Herman Kuhl was the soldier chastised by General George Patton during World War II
Decaset	Numerical combination of ten single numbers, number combinations or number patterns

Richard Andrew King

Decastack	Simultaneous numerical combination of ten numbers, number combinations or number patterns
Destiny	A predetermined course of events; same as fate
Dyad	A number composed of two digits
Elvis Presley	20th Century singer and performer; known as the King of Rock and Roll
Epochs	The three parts of a birth date. The 1st Epoch is the day, the 2nd Epoch is the month and the 3rd Epoch is the year
Expression (Exp)	That part of the Basic Matrix derived through addition of the numbers associated with the letters of a person's full name at birth; it is the personal profile of an individual describing his assets and liabilities
Fate	A predetermined course of events; same as destiny
Filter	The number (often not shown) through which the Influence number must pass to create the Reality number in an IR set; known also as a funnel
Fred Noonan	Amelia Earhart's navigator on their ill-fated flight
Genera	Letter groupings associated with the simple numbers 1 through 9
General George Patton	19th/20th Century American soldier
Grand Elemental	The number 9
Grand PC Couplet	the 3rd Pinnacle and Challenge pair; also known as the Grand Pinnacle/Challenge Couplet
Grand Pinnacle/Challenge Couplet	the 3rd Pinnacle and Challenge pair; also known as the Grand PC Couplet
Grant Sahib	Holy book of Sikhism
Guru Amardas	15th/16th Century saint and mystic
Hepset	Numerical combination of seven single numbers, number combinations or number patterns
Hepstack	Simultaneous numerical combination of seven numbers, number combinations or number patterns
Hexset	Numerical combination of six single numbers, number combinations or number patterns
Hexstack	Simultaneous numerical combination of six numbers, number combinations or number patterns

Homer	Greek author of the *Iliad* and the *Odyssey*; approx. 12th Century BC
Howard Hughes	20th Century American entrepreneur, industrialist, aviator and movie producer
Howland Island	An uninhabited coral island in the Central Pacific Ocean associated with the disappearance of Amelia Earhart and Fred Noonan
IR set	A numerical pattern or dyad showing the Influence energy (I) and its resulting Outcome or Reality energy (R)
Jan Patočka	20th Century Czech Philosopher
Johann Friedrich Von Schiller	18th/19th Century German poet, philosopher, historian, and playwright
John F. Kennedy	35th President of the United States of America
Keys of Fame	Dominant numerological components relating to a person's fame and fortune
Koran	Holy book of the Muslim religion
Letter Timeline (LTL)	The length of time given to the numerical value of each letter in a person's full birth name
Life Matrix	The internal framework of the Lifepath denoting time periods of a person's life and their fields of actions and outcomes
Lifepath (LP)	That part of the Basic Matrix derived through addition of a person's day, month and year of birth; describes the path of a person's life, its lessons and general field of activity; can also be seen as the script of a person's life or an energy world; designated as LP
Linkage	The continuous or repetitive occurrence of the same number, numbers, or number patterns in a chart; creates continuity
Linkage, Lifetime	Linkage existing from birth to death
Margaret Thatcher	Prime Minister of Great Britain, 1979 to 1990
Marilyn Monroe	20th Century American actress
Master Artistic Triad	The combination of master numbers 33, 66 and 99
Master number	A multiple digit number of the same single number or cipher such as 11, 333, or 7777
Master number 11	The *master aspirant/achiever* number
Master number 22	The *master builder/partner* number
Master number 33	The *master imaginator/communicator* number

Richard Andrew King

Master number 44	The *master worker/leader* number; also known as the generalship number
Master number 55	The *master explorer/creator* number
Master number 66	The *master lover/artisan* number
Master number 77	The *master thinker/revolutionary* number
Master number 88	The *master interactor/spiritual master* number
Master number 99	The *master performer/master's master* number
Material Nature (MN)	That part of the Basic Matrix describing a secondary layer of an individual's personality; derived by addition of the Nature and Lifepath
Material Soul (MS)	That part of the Basic Matrix describing a second level of needs, wants, desires and motivations; derived by addition of the Soul and Lifepath
Michael Jackson	20th Century American singer and entertainer
Muhammad Ali	20th Century American boxer
Name Timeline (NTL)	A person's full name subdivided into the separate names comprising the full name and designating a specific period of time based on the numerical value of each name
Nature	That part of the Basic Matrix describing a person's personality and nature of doing things; derived by addition of the consonants in the full birth name
Nonaset	Numerical combination of nine single numbers, number combinations or number patterns
Nonastack	Simultaneous numerical combination of nine numbers, number combinations or number patterns
Number 1	Rules the self, ego, identity, action, independence, logic and masculine energy
Number 2	Rules others, relationship, support, dependence, reaction, emotion and feminine energy
Number 3	Rules self-expression, image, health, words, children, sex, pleasure, communication
Number 4	Rules order, work, service, security, stability, roots, routines, convention and tradition
Number 5	Rules freedom and slavery, detachment, movement, motion, diversity, variety and the five senses; known as the Number of Man
Number 6	Rules personal love, the home, family, community, nurturing, romance and devotion

Number 7	Rules all things internal, study, thought, reclusion, introspection, secrecy, privacy, wisdom and folly
Number 8	Rules all things external, connection, disconnection, interaction, management, orchestration, manipulation
Number 9	Rules universality, philanthropy, education, theater, power and the public stage; known as the Number of Mankind
Number of Man	The number 5
Number of Mankind	The number 9; also known as the Grand Elemental
Numeric Houses	The numbers 1 through 9 associated with their particular letters
Octaset	Numerical combination of eight single numbers, number combinations or number patterns
Octastack	Simultaneous numerical combination of eight numbers, number combinations or number patterns
Oprah Winfrey	20th Century American entrepreneur, philanthropist, television host, actress, producer
PC Couplet	A Pinnacle and Challenge sharing the same timeline; also known as Pinnacle/Challenge Couplet
Performance/Experience (PE)	That part of the Basic Matrix describing the role a person will play in life; derived by addition of the Lifepath and Expression; designated as PE
Pinnacle #1	The Life Matrix number derived by addition of the day and month of birth
Pinnacle #2	The Life Matrix number derived by addition of the month and year of birth
Pinnacle #3	The Life Matrix number derived by addition of Pinnacles 1 & 2; known as the Grand Pinnacle; it is one-half of the core/center of a person's life; the other half is the Grand Challenge
Pinnacle #4	The Life Matrix number derived by addition of the day and year of birth; known as the Crown Pinnacle
Pinnacle/Challenge Couplet	A Pinnacle and Challenge sharing the same timeline; also known as Pinnacle/Challenge Couplet
Pinnacles	The four parts of the Life Matrix derived by addition; denotes activities that pull the person forward
Princess Diana	Diana Frances Spencer, Princess of Wales; international personality; mother of Prince William and Prince Harry; first wife of Prince Charles
Pythagoras	Greek philosopher, mathematician; 5th Century BC

Richard Andrew King

Quadset	Numerical combination of four single numbers, number combinations or number patterns
Quadstack	Simultaneous numerical combination of four numbers, number combinations or number patterns
Quaternary	A number composed of four digits
Quintset	Numerical combination of five single numbers, number combinations or number patterns
Quintstack	Simultaneous numerical combination of five numbers, number combinations or number patterns
Reincarnation	The process of a person being born in another body in another life
Saint Jagat Singh	20th Century saint and mystic
Saint Sawan Singh	19th/20th Century saint and mystic
Sarah Palin	20th Century American politician, commentator and author; former Governor of Alaska; first Republican woman nominated for the vice-presidency of the United States
Sikhism	Religion founded by Indian saint, Guru Nanak
Simple Letter Value Chart	A graphic representation or form showing the single numerical value of each letter in the English alphabet
Sir Isaac Newton	17th/18th Century English physicist, mathematician, astronomer, natural philosopher, alchemist, and theologian
Sir Winston Churchill	19th/20th Century British Prime Minister and leader
Soul	That part of the Basic Matrix derived from the numerical value of the vowels (A-E-I-O-U-Y) in the full birth name; describes needs, wants, desires and motivations
Specific Letter Value Chart	A graphic representation or form showing the specific numerical value of each letter in the English alphabet
Stacking	The simultaneous occurrence of the same number, numbers, or number patterns in a chart; creates intensity
Subcap	A number derived through subtraction of numbers in a group
The Kings Numerology™	A system of numeric analysis describing and defining the relationship between a person's natal data (full birth name and birth date) focused on the divine nature of numbers where God is King.
Timeline	A period of time indicating a start and stop point

Triad	A number composed of three digits
Triset	Numerical combination of three single numbers, number combinations or number patterns
Tristack	Simultaneous numerical combination of three numbers, number combinations or number patterns
Union Jack	National flag of Great Britain
USSR	Union of Soviet Socialist Republics
Voids	missing numbers in the full birth name of the individual; designated in a chart as "v"
Yang	Chinese word referencing male, masculine energy
Yin	Chinese word referencing female, feminine energy

INDEX

Richard Andrew King

RICHARD ANDREW KING
~ BOOKS ~
RichardKing.net and Major Online Retailers

The King's Book of Numerology (KBN1)
Volume 1-Foundations & Fundamentals

The King's Book of Numerology, Volume 1-Foundations & Fundamentals provides complete descriptions of Basic Numbers, Double Numbers, Purifier Numbers, Master Numbers, the Letters in Simple and Specific form as well as the Basic Matrix, the numerological blueprint of our lives.

"*The King's Book of Numerology* series contains new information that informs and predicts more completely and accurately than any previously published numerological work. It brings back the empowered sciences of long ago, information long since lost upon this plane."
~ G. Shaver

"The best numerology book I've ever read." ~ M.W.

"I've learned as much about numerology from *The King's Book of Numerology* the last few days than I have in my past five years of study." ~ Frank M.

The King's Book of Numerology II (KBN2)
Forecasting – Part 1

The King's Book of Numerology II: Forecasting – Part 1 is dedicated to opening the door to the divine blueprint of our lives. That plan, that divine blueprint of destiny, is exact, precise, unchangeable, unalterable and . . . knowable, at least in general terms.

Once this awareness of a predetermined fate becomes established through application of numbers and their truths, our understanding and consciousness of life will, no doubt, change. We will begin to see ourselves as part of an immense spiritual super-structure far beyond our current ability to comprehend, understand or perceive. Life will take on new meaning and, perhaps, we will even begin to awaken to greater spiritual truths. Subjects covered: Life Cycle Patterns, The Pinnacle/Challenge Matrix, Epoch Timeline, Voids, Case Studies and much more.

Richard Andrew King

The King's Book of Numerology 3 (KBN3)

Master Numbers

The King's Book of Numerology 3 – Master Numbers delves deeply into the subject of master numbers – multiple digit numbers of the same cipher, focusing especially on binary master numbers: 11-22-33-44-55-66-77-88-99.

Master numbers are the nuclear component of the numeric spectrum and play powerful roles in the destinies of individuals. They cannot be ignored.

KBN3 reveals the process of discovering hidden master numbers in all facets of a King's Numerology[tm] chart, how voids effect the life and much more.

The King's Book of Numerology 4 (KBN4)

Intermediate Principles

The King's Book of Numerology 4 – Intermediate Principles will expand your consciousness of the mysteries of life and destiny by taking you deeper into the secret world of numbers and their meaning.

Life is energy. People are energy. Numbers are arithmetic codes describing and defining the energies that comprise our lives and destinies. Like priceless treasures discovered during an archaeological dig, numbers and number patterns buried beneath the surface of single numbers contain a treasure trove of untold wealth and secret riches of knowledge and wisdom.

Intermediate Principles chapters include Common Names, Linkage, Stacking, Name Suffixes, Binary Capsets, Influence/Reality Set Formats, Dual Basic Matrix Components, Subcap Challenges, and much more.

The King's Book of Numerology 5 (KBN5)

I/R Sets – Level 1

IR SETS are the crux, core and substance of numerology forecasting, indispensable to the King's Numerology[tm] system and to anyone choosing to know where they've been, where they are now and where they're headed. They are obligatory for any serious and professional numerologist.

The King's Book of Numerology 5: I/R Sets – Level 1 offers a general explanation of each of the 81 IR Sets in order to create a foundation on which to build a greater understanding of how life's events affect us. KBN5 is a starting point from which to grow greater knowledge of one's self and destiny.

IR SETS are a gift for those willing to receive them, study them and apply their vast level of knowledge to make our lives more understandable, manageable, easier, better, whole.

The King's Book of Numerology 6 (KBN6)

Love Relationships

Note: This is a "stand alone" book. Its knowledge is not dependent on prior KBN publications.

The *King's Book of Numerology, Volume 6 – Love Relationships* (KBN6) guides you through this revolutionary method of understanding the Secrets of Love and Happiness via the mystical science of numbers. If you can add 1 + 1, you can quickly learn how to utilize and benefit from the great truths shared within this book.

The fundamental Secret of all great relationships, marriages and partnerships revolves around the quality and quantity of *Mutual Energetic Resonance* between the partners. This resonance (MER) is easily identified from the natal data of the individuals involved – their full birth names and birth dates. In fact, this birth data is where the mysteries of everything, including love relationships and destiny, all begins.

KBN6 is divided into two parts: Part 1 is the original book *Your Love Numbers*; Part 2 puts the King's Numerology[tm] number science to the test with twenty marital case studies broken into three segments: Section I. Marriages rated as excellent; Section II. Celebrity marriages ending in divorce; and Section III. Hollywood marriages that have endured. These case studies are powerfully insightful because they reveal, without question, the dramatic and irrefutable correlation between love and numbers.

Richard Andrew King

The King's Book of Numerology 7 (KBN7)

Parenting Wisdom

The King's Book of Numerology, Volume 7: Parenting Wisdom – Numerology & Life Truths (KBN7) is a compilation of two books in one. The reason for this is twofold: 1. To place the *Parenting Wisdom* series in one convenient resource; 2. As a continuing effort to place all King's Numerology™ books under one banner. KBN7 is also a "stand alone" book. Its knowledge is not dependent on having read prior KBN publications.

KBN7-Part 1: *Parenting Wisdom for the 21st Century – Raising Your Children by Their Numbers to Achieve Their Highest Potential* reveals the secrets to understanding a child's Basic Matrix and destiny through the most ancient of all sciences, numbers. Using numerology to help raise children is a revolutionary idea, reaping great rewards for children in helping them understand themselves, their life's journey and destiny.

KBN7-Part 2: *Parenting Wisdom – What to Teach the Children* offers thirty-three time-tested universal principles of life which parents can use to create a strong foundation for their children, allowing them to develop into whole, fulfilled and substantive adults. These thirty-three fundamental concepts offer parents a road map and paradigm of what to teach the children.

The King's Book of Numerology 8 (KBN8)

Forecasting, Part 2

The King's Book of Numerology, Volume 8 – Forecasting, Part 2 (KBN8) broadens and expands the knowledge of numerology forecasting into areas of greater depth and specificity, giving students and practitioners of this divine numeric science tools unknown heretofore, allowing them to rise to the zenith of understanding in decoding life and destiny, and once again proving that life is destined and that the blueprint of destiny is, indisputably, secretly hidden in our birth names and birth dates. Indeed, God did not drop us here without a plan or a way of knowing that plan if we so choose.

The King's Book of Numerology, Volume 8 – Forecasting, Part 2

Contents

The X-Y Paradigm, Cycle of Nines, Timeline Transitions, Lifetime Monthly Timeline (LMT), Annual Cycle Patterns – Monthly Timelines, Monthly Cycle Patterns (MCPs), Life Changes and the Number 5, Master Filters, Master Amalgams, Crown Roots/Pillars, Addresses – Homes and Businesses, Numerology Forecasting – Step-by-Step Analysis, and the 2016 Presidential Election Series – Articles: 1 to 10

The King's Book of Numerology, Volume 10: Historic Icons – Part 1

The King's Book of Numerology 9 (KBN9)

Numeric Biography – Princess Diana

The King's Book of Numerology, Volume 9 – Numeric Biography, Princess Diana was originally published as *Blueprint of a Princess – Diana Frances Spencer, Queen of Hearts*, in 1998 and reprised in 2017 – the 20th Anniversary of Diana's death – to be included in *The King's Book of Numerology Series.*

KBN9 thoroughly explains the life, destiny and heartbreak of Princess Diana based on the King's Numerology^{tm} and its system of numeric coding.

For a more thorough explanation, see the following *Blueprint of a Princess* description.

The King's Book of Numerology 10 (KBN10)

Historic Icons – Part 1

The King's Book of Numerology, Volume 10 – Historic Icons, Part 1 (KBN10) was initially published as *Destinies of the Rich & Famous – The Secret Numbers of Extraordinary Lives* and has been added to The King's Book of Numerology^{tm} series to expand its platform.

WHY do individuals become historic icons? What is it in their numbers allowing them to be rich or successful or famous or universally known globally and historically? Is it luck? Hard work? Advantage by family name? No. It is destiny, purely and simply, and the blueprint of that destiny is contained within the full birth name and birth date of each of these featured icons.

KBN10 highlights the following twelve famous historic individuals and offers explanations via The King's Numerology^{tm} as to why they have become globally historic figures – Dr. Albert Einstein, Amelia Earhart, Elvis Presley, General George Patton, Howard Hughes, John F. Kennedy, Marilyn Monroe, Michael Jackson, Muhammad Ali, Oprah Winfrey, Princess Diana and Sarah Palin.

Richard Andrew King

Blueprint of a Princess

Diana Frances Spencer - Queen of Hearts

The tragic death of Princess Diana of Wales - the most famous, the most photographed, the most written about woman of the modern world and possibly of all time - was one of the most shocking and saddening events of the late Twentieth Century. Not since the assassination of American President John Fitzgerald Kennedy in 1963, has such an event captured the attention of the world. On that ill-fated Sunday of 31 August 1997, and the following week until her funeral, there was much discussion and reflection of the Queen of Hearts, the People's Princess, England's Rose. But in all of the media news coverage, there was no discussion given to the cosmic aspects of her life and death.

Blueprint of a Princess is dedicated to addressing those issues through The King's Numerology[tm]. Its purpose and hope is to offer some consolation and explanation as to that one question so poignantly written on a card of condolence left with the multitude of flowers before the gates of Buckingham Palace. . . "Why?"

After learning from King's numerological teaching, it is impossible to conceive of going back to that 'twilight naive and foggy' state of being where one can only guess or hint at the truths, motivations and directions of one's life that are Pre-King. Not only do I recommend this book, but I suggest it and his other numerology books as absolutely necessary for the library of anyone even remotely interested in the science of numerology.

~ Hunter Stowers

99 Poems of the Spirit

99 Poems of the Spirit draws from the writings of Perfect Saints, Masters, Mystics and Sacred Scriptures. Designed to lift the consciousness, mind and heart, all of the poems are original works by Richard Andrew King. Their purpose is to help connect the reader with the mystic side of life in order to enhance the process of self-realization while advancing on the spiritual path and climbing the ladder leading to the ultimate attainment of God Realization. It is a treasure chest of poetic spiritual gems offered to excite, educate and stimulate the mind and soul in the glorious journey of spiritual ascent.

Messages from the Masters

Timeless Truths for Spiritual Seekers

In a time where there is more need for enlightenment than ever before, *Messages from the Masters: Timeless Truths for Spiritual Seekers* offers timeless truths for genuine seekers thirsty for spiritual nectar.

Masters are the PhDs of the universe, the Light Bearers of the Divine Flame. Their knowledge and wisdom are supreme. They have no equal. Although appearing human, they are not. Masters are the exalted Sons of God. Their chief duty is to rescue souls, liberating them from the maniacal maelstrom and madness of the material world and returning them to their eternal Home with the Lord.

Messages from the Masters is a rich source of hundreds of quotes from a cavalcade of nine Perfect Saints throughout the last six hundred years: Guru Ravidas, Kabir, Guru Nanak, Tulsi Sahib, Swami Ji Maharaj, Baba Jaimal Singh, Sawan Singh, Jagat Singh and Charan Singh. The messages in this book focus on the importance of the Divine Diet, the priceless Human Form, Reincarnation, the World, the Negative Power and Soul Food.

Warning! *Messages from the Masters* is not for the faint of heart or the worldly-minded. Masters come into the world to sever our attachment to it, not make it a paradise. Although the epitome of love and wisdom, they shoot straight from the hip, pull no punches, favor no religion. Their universal message of soul liberation is reflected in the statement of Saint Maharaj Charan Singh: *Just live in the creation and get out of it*!

The Age of the Female

A Thousand Years of Yin

The Age of the Female: A Thousand Years of Yin highlights the profound and extraordinary ascent of the female in the modern world, placing her center stage in the global spotlight as presidents and leaders of nations, titans of industry, corporate executives, military generals, media magnets, doctors, lawyers and a whole host of other prestigious titles normally associated with the male. Why has her rise to prominence been so rapid, especially in consideration of historic time? Why also has there been an increased interest in other people's lives in our society, in competitive athletics, personal data collection and the exploration of space and other worlds? *The Age of the Female: A Thousand Years of Yin* answers these questions. It is an insightful and exciting read into these mysteries, offering compelling and irrefutable evidence through the ancient science and art of numerology that, indeed, the age of the female has arrived and the next thousand years belong, not to him, but to her.

Richard Andrew King

The Age of the Female II
Heroines of the Shift

The Age of the Female II: Heroines of the Shift continues the remarkable journey of the female's ascent in the modern world of the 2nd Millennium. This installment is a general read in five chapters honoring the accomplishments of women in categories of female firsts, female Nobel laureates, female athletes, female icons and female quotations.

The achievements of the women featured in *The Age of the Female II: Heroines of the Shift* are deserving of respect and admiration. Their lives, challenges and successes are motivational catalysts for every individual to be the best he or she can be and to honor the very essence of what it is to be human. *The Age of the Female II: Heroines of the Shift* is intended to be an inspiring and educational read for everyone, not just women but men, too, offering knowledge and insight of the depth, power and daring-do of women as their Yin energy rises upon the global stage in this millennium which destiny has irrefutably marked as the Age of the Female.

Your Love Numbers
Discovering the Secrets of Your Life, Loves and Relationships

Your Love Numbers reveals the secret formula defining all great relationships and how to assess the love potential of any relationship in a matter of minutes.

Your Love Numbers teaches you how to assess a relationship or potential relationship in minutes, saving you endless time, energy, effort and possible heartache in the end. By knowing ourselves and the people we love, our relationships will be potentially more rewarding, satisfying, productive, peaceful, lasting and loving . . . for everyone - our family, spouses, partners, children, friends.

Your Love Numbers explains the mystery of love through the most ancient of all sciences . . . numbers, your numbers, calculated using only your full name and date of birth and those of the people you love! "Numbers rule the universe; everything is arranged according to number and mathematical shape," said Pythagoras. Everything - including light, sound and love can be measured in numbers! *Your Love Numbers* is based on thirty years of relationship research by master numerologist, Richard Andrew King. Applying his unique and revolutionary new theories, love and attraction between people can be determined using very easy to learn concepts. With a little study and practice, all this can be done in a minutes.

YourLoveNumbers.com

The Galactic Transcripts

The Galactic Transcripts will take you on a journey that is as provocative as it is mysterious. Its thirty-seven transmissions are channeled from a non-earth, alien group who identify themselves as members of the Space Brotherhood.

The Galactic Transcripts offer us descriptions of other worlds, their inhabitants, morals, ethics, and histories. They even forewarn of the coming cleansing of earth and the cataclysms preceding it. Other messages shed light on the original colonization of earth, telepathic communication, the power of love, the program of the Radiant One, and much more.

Those who have read *The Galactic Transcripts* have found them to be life-altering, profound, inspirational, transformative. Will they have that effect on you? Open your mind and allow the transcripts to take you beyond the limitations of our world and into new, undiscovered worlds far beyond our galaxy.

RichardKing.net
TheGalacticTranscripts.com

The Black Belt Book of Life
Secrets of a Martial Arts Master

The mystery and mystique of the martial arts is not only ages old, it's legend. Revered throughout the world, martial arts is a treasure chest of life secrets that transcend the boundaries of combat to include the expanse of life and living. Arguably, it is the greatest developmental system on earth for teaching the integration of body, mind and spirit

The Black Belt Book of Life: Secrets of a Martial Arts Master is not about physical fighting strategies and tactics. It is about concepts and principles we learn though martial arts training that can help us in the struggle of life, in the journey to conquer ourselves and gain the golden ring of our own completeness because in the end a true Black Belt should be a realized soul who, having engaged the enemy - himself - finds himself at the end of the journey, triumphant.

The Black Belt Book of Life: Secrets of a Martial Arts Master reveals many secrets of martial arts training, sharing these truths in quick and easy to read vignettes to benefit martial artists and the general public as well. It is a book for all readers, not just martial artists, both males and females, especially the youth of today who are in search of a foundation to guide their lives.

Richard Andrew King

The Karate Consciousness
From Worldly Warrior to Mystic Master

The Karate Consciousness – From Worldly Warrior to Mystic Master is dedicated to the philosophy that karate is both an excellent system for the integration of body, mind and spirit as well as an excellent vehicle for the evolution of one's consciousness of life from a mundane perspective to a more elevated and edified reality.

Just as many martial arts systems are comprised of an ascending ladder of colored belts to designate accomplishment, so life is also comprised of an ascending ladder of levels of consciousness from worldly to divine.

The Karate Consciousness – From Worldly Warrior to Mystic Master shares concepts and perspectives which may help the karate practitioner in climbing the "Ladder of Consciousness." Among such concepts are the Power in the Flock Syndrome, the Continuum, the D.C. Factor, the Great Law of Karma and much more.

Destinies of the Rich & Famous
The Secret Numbers of Extraordinary Lives

Why are rich and famous people rich and famous? Is it luck? Hard work? Advantage by family name? What makes them special? What secrets are the basis of their success?

Destinies of the Rich & Famous explores the secret numbers of the following famous global icons and explains through The King's Numerology[tm] why they are both rich and famous - Dr. Albert Einstein, Amelia Earhart, Elvis Presley, General George Patton, Howard Hughes, John F. Kennedy, Marilyn Monroe, Michael Jackson, Muhammad Ali, Oprah Winfrey, Princess Diana and Sarah Palin

Destinies of the Rich & Famous answers these questions and much more. Too, it reveals the clear correlation between a person's life and his or her natal data - the date of birth and full name of birth, illustrating the reality that fame and fortune and destined!

DestiniesOfTheRichAndFamous.com

Parenting Wisdom

Raising Your Children By Their Numbers
To Achieve Their Highest Potential

ParentingWisdom.net

This book is a must for any parent and all parents to be. It is vital to read this book now before you name your children. If you already have children, then it is just as important to understand them.

Richard Andrew King should be called Dr. King. His books are of the magnitude that will be read with reverence for generations to come. ~ Dr. Victoria Ford, J.D.

Parenting Wisdom for the 21st Century - Raising Your Children by Their Numbers to Achieve Their Highest Potential is a revolutionary addition to the process of arguably the most important job in the world, parenting.

The powerful information contained within this work will reveal the hidden desires driving your children, the paths they will follow in life, the roles they will give on the great life stage and much more – all designed to augment your parenting wisdom and support life's paramount parental purpose . . . to love the children and help them achieve their highest potential.

Parenting Wisdom 2

What To Teach The Children

This work is a companion book to *Parenting Wisdom For The 21st Century – Raising Your Children By Their Numbers To Achieve Their Highest Potential.*

Parenting is the most important and critical job in life because it encompasses the cultivating and sculpting of life itself as reflected in our children – the sanctity of life in manifest form.

In the process of parenting one of the most germane questions is, "What do we teach the children?" Parenting Wisdom offers thirty-three time-tested, universal principles which parents can use to create a strong foundation allowing children to develop into whole, fulfilled, and substantive adults.

The thirty-three principles include: The Five Needs of Children, Boundaries, Rules, And Regs, Your Life, Your Responsibility, Tender Love Versus Tough Love, The Four Cornerstones of a Substantive Life, The Temptations of S.A.D. (Sex, Alcohol, Drugs) and much more . . .

ParentingWisdom.net

Richard Andrew King

258

RICHARD ANDREW KING
~ CDs ~

RichardKing.net, CDBaby.com, and Online Retailers

Priceless Poetry & Prose 1
Dramatizations of Famous Literary Works

Wonderfully entertaining and educational artistic dramatizations of famous literary works for adults, children, teachers and students alike. Enjoy the timeless words of Shakespeare, Lincoln, Tennyson, Longfellow, Patrick Henry, Emily Dickinson, Chaucer and more.

Priceless Poetry & Prose 2
Selected Works of Edgar Allan Poe

Be enveloped in the mysterious and haunted world of one of America's most loved poets, Edgar Allan Poe. Highly entertaining and educational, enjoy classic poems such as, The Raven, Annabel Lee, Ulalume, Alone, Lenore and more.

Poems of the Spirit
Selected Original Poems of Richard Andrew King

A collection of original spiritual poems designed to edify the mind and uplift the spirit. Not for the faint of heart or worldly-minded, these works reflect timeless truths from scriptures, saints and mystics throughout the ages - messages enabling the individual to break the shackles of worldly ties in quest for spiritual realization.

Echoes from the Heart
Selected Original Songs of Richard Andrew King

An original collection of twelve of Richard's tug-at-your-heart ballads, cowboy songs, patriotic tributes and spiritual tunes for your soul. A few titles are *Waiting for You, Don't Forget the Heroes, One More Broken Heart, The Promise, Rodeo Cowboy, You Can't Push the River, No Itty Bitty Cowboy* and *Catch Me When I Fall*.

Richard Andrew King

ORDER INFORMATION

To order Books and CDs, go to
RichardKing.Net
or major online retailers

CONTACT

Richard Andrew King
PO Box 3621
Laguna Hills, CA 92654
RichardKing.Net
Rich @ RichardKing.net

NOTES

NOTES

NOTES

NOTES

NOTES

NOTES

NOTES

Made in the USA
Columbia, SC
07 January 2022